M000013142

SPIRITUAL LESSONS ALONG THE CAMINO:

A 40-Day Spiritual Journey

By Kim Brown

IMPRIMATUR:
Daniel Cardinal DiNardo,
Archbishop of Galveston-Houston

Spiritual Lessons along the Camino:

A 40-Day Spiritual Journey
By Kim Brown

Imprimatur: Daniel Cardinal DiNardo, Archbishop of Galveston-Houston

A member of the faculty at St. Thomas University at St. Mary's Seminary gave the *Nihil Obstat* for this book. The *Nihil Obstat* and *Imprimatur* are official declarations that this book is free of doctrinal or moral error.

Scripture references are taken from the New American Bible. Cover photo and photos in the book were taken by Kim Brown along the Camino de Santiago. Author back cover photo taken by a fellow pilgrim.

ISBN-13: 978-0615816661 (Brown)

First Edition, 2013

Printed in the United States of America

Author Acknowledgments

God has blessed me with amazing people in my life, and I am forever grateful for their love and support. Thanks to my family and friends for their prayers before, during, and after my pilgrimage.

To God, for giving me the blessings of this pilgrimage and the spiritual lessons I learned. May all the contents within be in accordance with His will. By His will and grace, may this book be used to help others along their faith journeys as pilgrims in this world.

Go to www.kimbrown.info to have Kim speak at your parish or for low-cost bulk distribution of this book at your parish or community.

Spiritual Lessons along the Camino

Introduction

"Whoever loves me will keep my word, and my Father will love him, and we will come to him and make our dwelling with him. Whoever does not love me does not keep my words; yet the word you hear is not mine but that of the Father who sent me. I have told you this while I am with you. The Advocate, the holy Spirit that the Father will send in my name—he will teach you everything and remind you of all that [I] told you. Peace I leave with you; my peace I give to you. Not as the world gives do I give it to you. Do not let your hearts be troubled or afraid." -John 14:23-28

Every day we each make many choices that impact our days, our lives, and the lives of others. Most of the time, we are not even conscious about how our decisions will impact ourselves, let alone others; yet everyday those decisions occur. This is part of my story about making a conscious decision to change my life and then allowing God to change it for me.

For me it was not a split-second decision to make drastic changes in my life, but one I had prayerfully considered over the course of two years. I had known God was calling me, but I was not sure where or what God was calling me to do. I definitely had a "case of Samuel," knowing I was being called but unsure where to go with that.

Scripture Meditation: 1 Samuel 3:3-10

"…..Samuel was sleeping in the temple of the Lord where the ark of God was. The Lord called to Samuel, who answered, "Here I am." He ran to Eli and said, "Here I am. You called me." "I did not call you," Eli said. "Go back to sleep." So he went back to sleep. Again the Lord called Samuel, who rose and went to Eli. "Here I am," he said. "You called me." But he answered, "I did not call you, my son. Go back to sleep." At that time Samuel was not familiar with the Lord, because the Lord had not revealed anything to him as yet. The Lord called Samuel again, for the third time. Getting up and going to Eli, he said, "Here I am. You called me." Then Eli understood that the Lord was calling the youth. So he said to Samuel, "Go to sleep, and if you are called, reply, 'Speak, Lord, for your servant is listening.'" When Samuel went to sleep in his place, the Lord came and revealed his presence calling out as before, "Samuel, Samuel!" Samuel answered, "Speak, for your servant is listening."

On many occasions I had felt God call me or urge me, but I was either unsure which way He wanted me to go, or I was afraid, so I stayed in my comfort zone. My comfort zone consisted of my career, my home, my family, and my friends. But similar to how God called Samuel multiple times, He continued to call me. Finally, I heard and understood God's call for my life. God called me to simplify and to get rid of all the excess and material things that trapped me and weighed me down. I was able to get rid of the majority of my possessions and then rent my home, which was much larger than a single person needed. In addition, God called me to radically change my life from working for a secular purpose in my career to working for His purpose and to help build His kingdom here on earth. I was not sure where God would take me, but I decided to quit my job and dispose of my belongings to go on a pilgrimage that would allow time away from the noise and distractions of everyday life and the people I love in order to hear God's voice more clearly.

I went on a pilgrimage to France, Spain, and Portugal. Part of that pilgrimage included the Camino de Santiago for forty days. My pilgrimage included opportunities to embrace the faith of those who came before me by visiting the places of some of my favorite Saints, as well as holy sites where Marian Apparitions have taken place. My pilgrimage included the following towns: Paris, Chartres, Lisieux, Mont Saint Michel, Lourdes, Fatima, Santarem, Avila, Madrid, Barcelona, Montserrat, as well as all the towns along the Camino. The Camino de Santiago (called "the Way of Saint James" in English) is a pilgrimage route in Europe that people have used for centuries. I walked the France route, which started at Saint Jean Pied de Port in the Pyrenees of France and concluded in Santiago de Compostela on the west coast of Spain.

During my time walking the Camino, I made an intentional decision to disconnect from talking back and forth with my family and friends. The only communication I had was letting them know I was alive and in what town. I did, however, continue to read their prayer requests and spent a good amount of time during my walk praying for those I cared for who were back home. I wanted to spend my forty days on the Camino with God, blocking out the thoughts of others. Part of the reason for my pilgrimage and disconnection was to identify God's will for my life and what vocation He desired for me: a married life, a religious life, or a committed single life. I have always been a goal-oriented, driven person, so knowing my vocation and focusing on my ministry within that vocation seemed like the thing I should be focusing on to best serve God. I wanted to use the opportunity to hear God and follow His will for my life.

The joke goes, "Want to make God laugh? Just tell Him your plans!" I had my plan of discovering my vocation. There I was again being goal oriented, but I have since learned that God had other plans. During my entire pilgrimage, the spiritual lessons I received constantly amazed me. Some seemed very simple, while others were truly complex to me. In addition, I found that Bible passages I had heard before took on new meanings when I heard them or meditated on them again. By God's grace, without the distractions and noise of everyday life, I heard God speaking to me. It was never in a voice-from-the-sky way, but usually I would feel led to do something. The Holy Spirit was guiding me, and because I had turned the entire trip over to God, I made myself open to hearing the movement of the Holy Spirit within my innermost being. It was truly amazing, for never in my life had I heard God so much!

Walking the Camino is not a race, and because I was not under any pressure of a timeline or flight back home, I was able to walk and enjoy my experience instead of calculating what town I needed to get to each day. In addition, I had not read a guidebook ahead of time about the Camino, nor did I even bring a guidebook. Prior to leaving the states, I spent three hours looking at a European map and planning in what order I would visit the various towns. I also wrote down the various town names and distance between each town. Other than that, I left the planning up to God and was on His timeline. I literally just showed up in Saint Jean Pied de Port and began walking, following the shells, yellow arrows, and red and white stripes that marked the trail.

Something I had not expected while walking was the fellowship of the Camino. People from all over the world were hiking the Camino, and although we came from many countries with many languages, I was able to communicate with many people. I had intentionally disconnected from relationships back home, but I knew God had intentionally brought these new relationships into my life for a reason. My time on the Camino was not a silent, forty-day pilgrimage but instead was a healthy balance. The majority of the walk was in silence, but I would share in fellowship and conversation at the pilgrim's lodging places when we were breaking bread.

Finally, as mentioned before, with my mind solely focused on God, and my inner self being quiet, I was able to hear

God more than at any other time in my life, and I began noticing spiritual insights He was giving me. While walking for six to ten hours a day, I began to record those thoughts on my camera for myself because I did not want to forget them. Then somewhere along the way, I realized they were not just spiritual insights for me, but they were meant for me to share. I knew this was where God was calling me to work for His church as part of the new evangelization. What I am going to share with you will not be new for all of you, but it may give you a new understanding on many components of the Christian faith. The following chapters include the spiritual lessons that richly enhanced my pilgrimage along the Camino de Santiago and continue to enhance my spiritual life. May it hopefully enhance your spiritual life, and may you hear the Holy Spirit calling you!

Lesson 1

On the day I hiked from Saint Jean Pied de Port to Roncesvalles, I was amazed to see how many fellow pilgrims there were. I was hiking during the off-season of the Camino (many hikers go in the summer months), yet the entire day, fellow pilgrims constantly passed us, or we passed them. Each time pilgrims passed, they joyfully shouted the words, "Buen Camino," a rallying cry of the pilgrims that means, "Good way." Out of the twenty-seven kilometers that day, only during the last four kilometers did the crowd die down. This was probably because fellow hikers were walking much faster or much slower than my companions I had met on the train and me. In Roncesvalles there were over three hundred pilgrims in the *albergue* (bunkhouses for pilgrims), and many people stayed in the private accommodations. Roncesvalles, which is the first town in Spain on the route, is a common starting place for people who want to avoid the challenging walk from Saint Jean Pied de Port. Irish pilgrims I met, who had hiked multiple Camino routes, told me that the walk from Saint Jean over the Pyrenees was the physically hardest of any Camino route they had walked.

Everyone felt excitement for this new adventure that would be the next month of his or her life. The excitement was so overwhelming that, in addition to seeing the pilgrims, I could also hear them. It was after Pamplona, Spain, that the numbers of pilgrims seemed to dwindle, and hikers entered into a silent state on the trail. There was still friendly encouragement, but I think everyone became conscious and respected the silence of the Camino. It was in that silence that I first came to appreciate time to think, to pray, and to have quiet reflection. We spend so much of our lives in noise—noise from people, noise from work, noise from school, noise from hobbies, noise from ministries, noise from computers, noise from phones, and noise from radios, and the list goes on. Noise is one of the greatest allies of the devil. If we are simply distracted from the noise, then we are unable to solely focus on God. Noise does not always come from an evil source, for we could be listening to Christian music. If a noise distracts us from focusing on God, then that noise is to our detriment instead of our advantage.

During that first part of walking, I began to love the silence that the trail offered. I was able to meditate on the Stations of the Cross (our Lord's passion) and the twenty mysteries of the rosary, to pray for my family and friends, and to just be silent in God's presence.

In our spiritual lives, we need to cut out the noise and distractions of our own lives. Find where noise is coming from, and ask yourself if you can cut something out. In my career others knew me for maximizing my time to get tasks accomplished, and I taught time management (which is really all about "you management"). People often told me, "I have no free time." After I sat down with them, we could find twenty to forty hours of poorly spent time in their weeks. Not all of us are called to a religious life in a contemplative order, but God does call each of us to a contemplative life with Him. How much time are you giving God each week to simply be with Him? Not doing for Him, as in service projects (yes, He calls us to service, but first He wants us), but in just being with Him through prayer, silence, meditation, and reflection. It is at this point that the majority of us will realize we can do better. If you honestly examine your day and week, I think you will be amazed with the noise in your life that does not need to be there. What noise are you willing to cut out for God? The radio on your car ride to work? Going out to eat on your lunch break? Television? Movies? Sporting games? Fiction books? Poker night? Date night? Sleeping in? Social media? Internet?

In my career, I was very busy. I had distinguished myself at a young age and was constantly working to improve my department. Usually, I would get home sometime after dark and, literally, get ready for bed upon arriving home, but I always turned on a movie to watch as I fell asleep. Then one day I was challenged, as I am challenging you now. Watching a movie in and of itself is not a vice, but I realized I spent fourteen hours a week watching movies yet did not spend fourteen hours a week with God. Something had to change. Fact is, my Netflix subscription dropped dramatically! Ironically, as a time-management person, I liked watching a movie over television. I knew exactly how long a movie would be on, while with TV shows, I sometimes got dragged in to the next show, and next thing I knew, three hours had gone by.

I am not asking you to cut out all of the noise and distractions from your life; I am simply asking you to honestly evaluate your life and say, "God, I am going to give you this because I love you." If you love someone, you want to spend time with him or her. I know God loves you, and He is waiting for you. He loves you so much that He will meet you wherever you are. You do not have to drive a long distance to be with Him—though He does love it when you come to His house for dinner (the banquet of the Mass). He is waiting each minute of each day for you, and He is ready for a deeper relationship. What are you willing to give up to meet Him in silence for prayer, meditation, and reflection?

Scripture Meditation: Luke 10:38-42

As they continued their journey he entered a village where a woman whose name was Martha welcomed him. She had a sister named Mary [who] sat beside the Lord at his feet listening to him speak. Martha, burdened with much serving, came to him and said, "Lord, do you not care that my sister has left me by myself to do the serving? Tell her to help me." The Lord said to her in reply, "Martha, Martha, you are anxious and worried about many things. There is need of only one thing. Mary has chosen the better part and it will not be taken from her."

Reflection:

What noise kept Martha from being able to be with the Lord?

When in my life have I been so busy trying to serve God that I failed to be with God?

What noise in my life is currently keeping me from spending time with God?

Now the good news: for those of us who are service-oriented people, always working for the Lord but not always taking time to be with the Lord, we can change. It does not mean we stop serving. But to truly serve others with the love of God, we need to be filled with the love of God! Martha's story continues when we read John 11:17-27.

When Jesus arrived, he found that Lazarus had already been in the tomb for four days. Now Bethany was near Jerusalem, only about two miles away. And many of the Jews had come to Martha and Mary to comfort them about their brother. When Martha heard that Jesus was coming, she went to meet him; but Mary sat at home. Martha said to Jesus, "Lord, if you had been here, my brother would not have died. [But] even now I know whatever you ask of God, God will give you." Jesus said to her, "Your brother will rise, in the resurrection on the last day." Jesus told her, "I am the resurrection and the life; whoever believes in me, even if he dies, will live, and everyone who lives and believes in me will never die. Do you believe this?" She said to him, "Yes, Lord. I have come to believe that you are the Messiah, the Son of God, the one who is coming into the world."

We see a changed Martha. She hears the Lord is coming, and this time, instead of preparing the house and tending to the mourning guest, she runs to the Lord. Are you ready to abandon your to-do list and all that noise so you can run to the Lord in complete trust and faith?

Lesson 2

Initially along the Camino, I prayed the Stations of the Cross to think about the great sacrifice that Jesus made to pay for a debt I could never repay and one that he did not owe. The stations gave me a way to meditate on the love our Lord has for us as well as helped me to put my small amount of pain into proportion. Yes, my bag was heavy but not as heavy as the cross Christ had to carry. Yes, it might be hot or cold, but at least I had the proper garments to wear. Yes, I was thirsty and some days drank four liters of water while I was walking, but at least I had access to good, clean water. From my first day until my last day on the Camino, the Stations of the Cross helped me to grow spiritually. In addition, the Stations became part of my language with fellow pilgrims.

The first station has Christ being sentenced to death by Pilate, and I see myself as Pilate. How many times have I failed under the attack of peer pressure? How many times have I not stood up for God or what was right because I was afraid of going against the crowd? It is in this Station that I am able to see my failures and my weaknesses.

Scripture Meditation: Matthew 27:15-26

Now on the occasion of the feast the governor was accustomed to release to the crowd one prisoner whom they wished. And at that time they had a notorious prisoner called [Jesus] Barabbas. So when they had assembled, Pilate said to them, "Which one do you want me to release to you, [Jesus] Barabbas or Jesus called Messiah?" For he knew that it was out of envy that they had handed him over. While he was still seated on the bench, his wife sent him a message, "Have nothing to do with that righteous man. I suffered much in a dream today because of him." The chief priests and the elders persuaded the crowds to ask for Barabbas but to destroy Jesus. The governor said to them in reply, "Which of the two do you want me to release to you?" They answered, "Barabbas!" Pilate said to them, "Then what shall I do with Jesus called Messiah?" They all said, "Let him be crucified!" But he said, "Why? What evil has he done?" They only shouted the louder, "Let him be crucified!" When Pilate saw that he was not succeeding at all, but that a riot was breaking out instead, he took water and washed his hands in sight of the crowd, saying, "I am innocent of this man's blood. Look to it yourselves." And the whole people said in reply, "His blood be upon us and upon our children." Then he released Barabbas to them, but after he had Jesus scourged, he handed him over to be crucified. Then the soldiers of the governor took Jesus inside the praetorium and gathered the whole cohort around him.

Reflection:

When have I allowed others to influence a decision and gone against what I knew to be right?

When have I failed to act on behalf of God?

So often when we read the Bible, we tend to look at people as either good or bad, but the reality is we all have good and bad in ourselves. The issue of good versus evil is not an exterior battle but an interior battle within our very hearts. Like Peter, I have failed our Lord and have denied knowing Him when I have failed to do His will or stand up for Him. But like Peter, God has also given me forgiveness, as well as given me the Holy Spirit. My goal is to always speak the truth in love, which may anger people, but I would rather be hated by man than crucify my God, who has suffered enough because of my failings.

Lesson 3:

While walking the Camino, I noticed a difference in my prayers regarding my pain and injuries. Before this pilgrimage, when I had an injury, I would ask God to remove the pain and to heal me. Yet, very early on in my pilgrimage, as I walked and felt pain in different parts of my body, I used a very different prayer. First, I offered that small amount of pain up to God as a sign of my love for Him and atonement for my sins. I then asked God to take away the pain if it was His will but if I needed the pain to grow spiritually, to give me His grace to accept it. Some days, almost immediately, the pain would disappear, and other days I continued with the physical pain. That simple prayer helped me grow spiritually from viewing God as a "genie God," granting me my wishes, to viewing God as "my God," the Lord of my life.

Scripture Meditation: Matthew 26:38-42

Then he said to them, "My soul is sorrowful even to death. Remain here and keep watch with me." He advanced a little and fell prostrate in prayer, saying, "My Father, if it is possible, let this cup pass from me; yet, not as I will, but as you will." When he returned to his disciples he found them asleep. He said to Peter, "So you could not keep watch with me for one hour? Watch and pray that you may not undergo the test. The spirit is willing, but the flesh is weak."

Reflection:

When bad things happen, do I ask God to remove them or do I ask for His will?

How can praying for God's will offer me comfort?

So much of our culture is about comforts and pleasure, but usually our growth occurs during our trials. Think of Peter's trial during the Lord's sentencing. That trial caused Peter the growth he needed—from overconfidence in himself to confidence in Jesus.

Lesson 4:

The landscape of the Camino is absolutely breathtaking. While in God's creation, enjoying the splendor He created, I took notice of the wild fruit that grew along the path. Out in the middle of nowhere grew wild blackberries, elderberries, raspberries, and an occasional fig tree. These wild fruits intertwined among other plants, weeds, and thorns. Sometimes the amount of soil was so sparse in rocky areas, I had to question how the fruit survived.

At first, I was hesitant to try the wild fruit, because I was traveling alone, but every now and then, I would give in and try some. It often only took one bite for me to decide the fruit was bad and to avoid trying any more for a few days. After eating one piece of fruit in particular, I had to immediately spit it out and take a drink of water. Then I had to spit the water out as well, trying to clean out my mouth. The taste of the fruit, though it was the right color and appeared ripe, was horrible and bitter. It tasted so bad that I thought I might have eaten a poisonous berry.

Vineyards that grew along the route appeared well maintained, and by their massiveness, I knew they were for wine production. The grapes in the vineyards looked tempting, but knowing this was someone's property, I could not take them without feeling guilty for stealing from someone's livelihood. However, I was lucky enough to be hiking the Camino during harvest time, so the markets were full of local grapes, and many towns were holding their annual wine festivals to coincide with the harvest. The grapes I purchased were delicious.

One day, God had me take notice of two very different pictures. On the left side of the trail, I saw wild blackberries that had turned the right color, but they were not even the size of a dime, growing alongside weeds, thorns, and bushes. In addition, the dirt on that side was mixed in with rocky ground. In contrast, the right side of the trail had gorgeous vineyards. The vines were full and lush, and the grape clusters were picture perfect. The carefully tended vineyard had good soil without weeds. I thought of the irony of how only a four-foot-wide path separated these two contrasting sides.

This thought, of course, led me to think and understand more fully the parable about the sower that Jesus shared with His followers. Think about going to church and hearing the word of God proclaimed by your pastor. Some of us would leave feeling inspired, but as time went by, the temporary motivation to live our lives according to God's way would diminish. To truly allow the word of God to change our lives on a continuous basis, we must prepare our hearts, minds, and bodies to not only receive the word, but to allow it to fully encompass our lives. We must be gardeners, weeding our own gardens (our thoughts and actions) so that the word of God can flourish in our gardens. We need to pull out the rocks that cause us to stumble and prevent us from having good soil to grow in. We must pull weeds that are the various vices or noises in our lives that choke out the word of God from our minds and hearts. Finally, we must ensure that our roots are able to grow deep in knowledge and desire of God. We can do this by praying more and reading our Bibles more to allow our roots to grow deep inside the good soil God has ready for us.

Scripture Meditation: Matthew 13:18-23

"Hear then the parable of the sower. The seed sown on the path is the one who hears the word of the kingdom without understanding it, the evil one comes and steals away what was sown in his heart. The seed sown on rocky ground is the one who hears the word and receives it at once with joy. But he has no root and lasts only for a time. When some tribulation or persecution comes because of the word, he immediately falls away. The seed sown among thorns is the one who hears the word, but then worldly anxiety and the lure of riches choke the word and it bears no fruit. But the seed sown on rich soil is the one who hears the word and understands it, who indeed bears fruit and yields a hundred or sixty of thirtyfold."

Reflection:

What are some stumbling blocks that I need to remove from my life? And how can I remove them?

What are some vices that I need to remove?

What are some ways I can expand my roots to know and love God more?

How can I tend to my spiritual garden to nourish the soil?

In Genesis, Chapter 2:15, we see that man's first responsibility was to cultivate and keep the garden of Eden. "*The Lord God then took the man and settled him in the garden of Eden, to cultivate and to care for it.*"

The first responsibility given to Adam also needs to be our first responsibility today. We need to focus on keeping our gardens tilled to keep out the things that will hinder our lives with God. God gave us rich soil, but it is our responsibility to keep that soil rich and clean. Allowing in a few weeds can quickly turn into a garden full of weeds.

Lesson 5:

As mentioned before, I had left my life to follow God and discover God's will for me. It was on the Camino de Santiago—the Way of Saint James—that I realized I was not on the Way of Saint James but the Way of Kim, Camino de Kim. I was on the path to discover whom it was God was calling me to be. We each are given a path in life that God calls us to follow, and He waits for each of us to respond. Our faith journeys do not begin the day we decide to love and serve God; our stories begin the very moment our lives begin. Every event and person I've come across has helped to shape my faith story. Even the people who led me away from God have shaped my faith journey. Saint Augustine would have never been the man of God he grew to be had he not fallen so far away from God. In the same sense, people like Saint Therese of Lisieux did not need to fall away from God to become the girl and young woman of God that she became in her lifetime. No two paths to God will ever be the same, but we each have a path to God. We only need to look at the past, realize how the past leads to the present, and realize how the past and present will lead to our futures. My hope is that the Camino de Kim leads me everyday closer to God.

Scripture Meditation: Acts 9:1-22

Now Saul, still breathing murderous threats against the disciples of the Lord, went to the high priest and asked him for letters to the synagogues in Damascus, that, if he should find any men or women who belonged to the Way, he might bring them back to Jerusalem in chains. On his journey, as he was nearing Damascus, a light from the sky suddenly flashed around him. He fell to the ground and heard a voice saying to him, "Saul, Saul, why are you persecuting me?" He said, "Who are you, sir?" The reply came, "I am Jesus, whom you are persecuting. Now get up and go into the city and you will be told what you must do." The men who were traveling with him stood speechless, for they heard the voice but could see no one. Saul got up from the ground, but when he opened his eyes he could see nothing; so they led him by the hand and brought him to Damascus. For three days he was unable to see, and he neither ate nor drank.

There was a disciple in Damascus named Ananias, and the Lord said to him in a vision, "Ananias." He answered, "Here I am, Lord." The Lord said to him, "Get up and go to the street called Straight and ask at the house of Judas for a man from Tarsus named Saul. He is there praying, and [in a vision] he has seen a man named Ananias come in and lay [his] hands on him, that he may regain his sight." But Ananias replied, "Lord, I have heard many sources about this man, what evil things he has done to your holy ones in Jerusalem. And here he has authority from the chief priests to imprison all who call upon your name." But the Lord said to him, "Go, for this man is a chosen instrument of mine to carry my name before Gentiles, kings, and Israelites, and I will show him what he will have to suffer for my name." So Ananias went and entered the house; laying his hands on him, he said, "Saul, my brother, the Lord has sent me, Jesus who appeared to you on the way by which you came, that you may regain your sight and be filled with the holy Spirit." Immediately things like scales fell from his eyes and he regained his sight. He got up and was baptized, and when he had eaten, he recovered his strength. He stayed some days with the disciples in Damascus and he began at once to proclaim Jesus in the synagogues, that he is the Son of God. All who heard him were *astounded and said, "Is not this the man who in Jerusalem ravaged those who call upon this name, and came here expressly to take them back in chains to the chief priests?" But Saul grew all the stronger and confounded [the] Jews who lived in Damascus, proving that this is the Messiah.*

Reflection:

As a chosen instrument of God, how does my past play a role in sharing my faith with others?

How do my past and present sins cause others to question or doubt my sincerity to serve God?

In the Bible, we not only learn about Paul's willingness to follow God, but we also learn the story of a fourteen-year-old girl (Mary) and her willingness to do God's will. If we are willing to give God our lives, He will truly use us to do amazing things. God created us, and He has chosen us to be His instruments, but He gives us the option to say yes or no. When we say yes to God, the outcomes are far greater than we could ever imagine. Let each one of us have the faith and trust that Mary had when she spoke these words found in Luke 1:38: "*Behold, I am the handmaid of the Lord. May it be done to me according to your word.*"

Lesson 6:

The common language on the Camino was English. I was surprised by how many fellow pilgrims spoke English and how that allowed us to share with each other. The pilgrims I met came from many backgrounds, countries, and religions, but we all shared the experience of hiking the Camino. I spent my time walking the Camino mainly in silence, allowing God to fill me up. Once I stopped walking, I spent a good amount of my time using what God had given me for others. I had many meaningful conversations with pilgrims, from short chats while putting boots on in the mornings to long conversations in our bunks in the afternoons.

In life, we spend so much time and so many conversations on superficial things—topics that are safe for us to share—and do not put our personal selves out there too far. When we meet new people, the questions and conversations often sound like this: What's your name? Where are you from? What do you do? Are you married? Do you have children? How is the weather? Where do you go to school? These questions by themselves and the amount of information we typically share do not require us to share our innermost thoughts, dreams, and fears—we do not even scratch the surface of who we are. We call these questions "small talk." I do not know where the term small talk came from, but my guess is we call it small talk because it reveals nothing "big" about ourselves! On the other hand, the first question usually asked on the Camino is, "Why are you hiking?" This question immediately cuts to the core of who we are and gives some big answers to who we are.

I met and had meaningful conversations with pilgrims. I had multiple ten–minute, one-time conversations with others. Other pilgrims I would see over my entire pilgrimage off and on again and share hour-long conversations. I was able to build relationships with those pilgrims. In all those cases, I had the opportunity to be a witness to my faith and my God. Many people I met were hiking to find themselves, which is something that humans have always been searching for. Finding ourselves is not a twenty-first century invention; it has been around since the beginning of humankind. The goal of finding ourselves is a deception given to us by the devil. For if we spend time trying to find ourselves, then we are not spending time finding God. We spend that time chasing pursuits to make ourselves happy, and we miss the peace and joy that God created for us.

I had thought that the majority of people hiking the Camino would be on a pilgrimage for spiritual reasons. The majority of people I met were hiking for vacation, adventure, or change in life. Even though their original intentions were not for making spiritual pilgrimages, hikers had too much alone time to not reflect on life and to not think about God. In addition, the trail wove past a church, even when out of the way, in every town we walked through. The Camino trail itself was constantly calling us to God, and like the towns themselves—designed with a church in the middle—we were being called to put God in the center of our lives.

I remember in particular one night a conversation I had with a German man. We each were on our own bunk bed, and he asked me why I was hiking. I shared my story about some of the life changes I had made and that I was hiking to discern God's will for my life. The German then shared why he was hiking. He was a recent college graduate but did not want to go to work in the area he had studied. He decided to take a holiday to find himself. I remember saying something along the lines of, "That is the difference; you hike the Camino to find yourself, while I hike to find God's will for me." Although I am not that much older than the German, I had graduated college ten years before him. I had spent a good amount of my life chasing things that would make me happy—you know, all those things we call the American dream! All that chasing and I finally realized none of that made me truly happy— that true happiness is lasting and gives us peace and joy. Sure, getting a dream job, an award, a pay raise, a new car, a home, and all those other things might give us short-term happiness, but happiness in "possessions and things" does not last, because we want more things when the last thing no longer brings us happiness. But when we seek God's will for our lives and then we actually follow it, we are able to find peace and joy that nothing can match. When we try to find ourselves, we get lost in selfishness. On the other hand, when we seek God and His will for our lives, we will find Him in everything, including ourselves.

Scripture Meditation: 1 John 2:15-17

Do not love the world or the things in the world. If anyone loves the world, the love of the Father is not in him. For all that is in the world, the sensual lust, enticement for the eyes, and a pretentious life, is not from the Father but is from the world. Yet the world and its enticement are passing away. But whoever does the will of God remains forever.

Reflection:

In what ways do I seek to love God or myself more?

Through my conversations with other people, is it obvious that I love God? If not, how can I make it obvious?

In our society, this is one of the greatest challenges. We are constantly being assaulted with "I want." I want this; I want that. We are kids at Christmas screaming, "Me. Me. Me." Of course, it does not stand out or seem that strange, because our entire society is doing it, so the I-thought process has become the new normal. We have commercials that tell us we should have it. Our friends tell us we deserve it. Through our entire lives, these little messages begin to grow on us so much that we believe them. What do I want? This is just another one of the devil's deceptions.

Romans 12:2 challenges, "*Do not conform yourself to this age but be transformed by the renewal of your mind, that you may discern what is the will of God, what is good and pleasing and perfect.*" I have to challenge myself daily, and now I challenge you to do the same. Let's cause the devil to panic. Let's quit seeking ourselves and making ourselves happy and begin seeking God's will for our lives to gain the peace and joy God has planned for us!

Lesson 7:

Hiking the Camino de Santiago was one of the physically hardest things I have ever done. To add to the challenge, the weather would shift, creating difficult environments. The weather shifted from me needing my winter coat while sleet came over the mountains to me sweating while walking in shorts and a T-shirt. In addition, my body suffered physical injuries, from blisters all over my feet to a pulled groin muscle. Yet, it was one day walking in the mountains with rocks all about me that God made one of my spiritual reflections come to life. A few years back, I had led a spiritual reflection for a group of women about stumbling blocks and stepping-stones. Walking the Camino truly helped me understand the concepts that I had previously spoken about.

You see, we often face hardships and challenges. Sometimes these come out of nowhere, and we trip over stumbling blocks and fall down. Other times we see stumbling blocks on paths ahead of us (and our friends even warn us about them), yet we keep walking and thinking that somehow the stumbling blocks will move themselves. Once again, we hit stumbling blocks and fall down. If we were to look back on our lives, we would see those stumbling blocks often gave us chances to rise up and go on to new heights. Those stumbling blocks become our stepping-stones. The wisest people learn from their mistakes. If I stumble along the Christian path and fall into sin, I have three choices: continue sinning and fall harder, do nothing and have a pity party, or rise up and ask for God's grace to conquer the sin that caused me to stumble. At different times in my life, I have responded to sin in each of those three choices. But I can tell you that it is the third choice I strive to do. It is the only one that brings me peace and comfort. Every obstacle and challenge we face, if we allow it, will help us grow in our spiritual lives.

Each day as I walked, I would often meditate on the Stations of the Cross, the Lord's passion. After Jesus was killed, Christians would make a pilgrimage to Jerusalem and walk in the footsteps of our Lord's passion. Upon Jerusalem not being safe for Christians, the Church began offering various Stations of the Cross for Christians to make their own pilgrimages at their own churches. The Stations recount the tradition of Jesus falling three times on his way to his death, carrying the cross. It was during one of my meditations that I thought our Lord himself had stumbling blocks: He physically fell down, he received a beating, and the weight of the cross was so great, his human body could not stand. Yet, after each fall, he rose up again. Jesus Christ, rising up after falling from the weight of the cross, gives us hope; he turns the stumbling block into a stepping-stone.

Scripture Meditation: Proverbs 24:16

For the just man falls seven times and rises again, but the wicked stumble to ruin.

Reflection:

In my life what has been a stumbling block that turned into a stepping-stone?

How can meditating on the Lord's passion strengthen me to rise when I stumble?

Take comfort knowing that each time you stumble, God will give you the grace to rise again. Through His mercy and compassion, my stumbling blocks have become the stepping-stones that I currently stand on. On the Camino, I could have allowed the pain to be my stumbling block and quit, but instead I kept walking through the pain, and that pain went from being a stumbling block to a stepping-stone for spiritual growth.

Lesson 8:

One day as I walked through the vineyards, I had time to reflect on the vineyards and the harvest. I was passing through the vineyards while the laborers were out picking grapes from the branches. Many towns were celebrating the harvest with their annual wine festivals.

The vineyards were massive and stretched as far as the eye could see. I saw a truck transporting about six field hands for picking the grapes. That instantly brought to mind the parable of our Lord telling us the harvest is bountiful, but the laborers are few. I thought about my time on the Camino and how easy it was, when speaking with fellow pilgrims, to share my story and how God was working in my life with them. Just simply sharing my story and the reason I was walking the Camino gave me the opportunity to share God's story. The majority of the people I spoke with would not classify themselves as Christians, yet I had no problem sharing God with them.

Before I went on this pilgrimage, how often did I fail to share with others what God was doing in my life? How often in my conversations at work, with friends, at the store, and everywhere I went, did I fail to talk about God and the grace He has given through His son? Why did I not share with others the greatest gift I had ever been given? Jesus told us, 'the harvest is bountiful and the laborers are few.' And now we know why. I, like so many of my fellow brothers and sisters in Christ, failed to share God's love with everyone we met.

Now society tells us that talking about politics and religion is not polite and can cause arguments, as well as cause us to lose friends. On the Camino, I met people with very different views on religion, morals, and beliefs, and sharing my faith did not cause them to distance themselves. In reality, it attracted them even more to me. One morning I met a woman as we were preparing to depart the albergue, and we shared our stories on why we were hiking. She shared that she was agnostic and put up a little barrier. At the end of that ten-minute conversation, I wished her and the other pilgrims, "Buen Camino," and told them I was going to go to morning prayers and Mass at the convent in town. She asked if she could come with me and we went to the chapel. I explained certain parts to her and let her use my missal so she could have the readings in English, as the Mass was in Spanish. At the end of Mass, we left the chapel, and she invited me for a drink. We went to a café and continued talking for an hour before we parted ways. I would only see the woman once more on my pilgrimage. We saw each other in Santiago at the Mass.

You see, we have brothers and sisters walking around this world, and they are lost. They are searching. They think they are searching for happiness, and they try many things to make themselves happy, but none has a lasting impact. I am sure we could each name things we once upon a time tried to make ourselves happy with that did not give us the lasting joy God created us for. Once we find what God never intended to have hidden from us—Himself—we have eternal joy. Now this is where Jesus calls us to share that eternal joy with others.

When I was looking at buying a house, my brother recommended going to a different neighborhood because I could get a much bigger house for less money than the neighborhood I was originally looking in. I went to the recommended neighborhood, saved $30,000, and ended up with about three hundred square feet more. When we know something is good, we want to share that with the people we love. In the same way, we know God is good, so why would we not want to share that with people we love. Well, for most of us, we share our faith with our families and friends, but remember we are called to love our neighbors, and Christ clearly tells us our neighbors are everyone. We are called to love everyone we meet as if we are loving Christ, himself. So in that context, we know God is good, and we are called to share this with everyone we meet because, as true disciples of Christ, we love everyone.

Scripture Meditation: Luke 10:1-2

After this the Lord appointed seventy [-two] others whom he sent ahead of him in pairs to every town and place he intended to visit. He said to them, "The harvest is abundant but the laborers are few; so ask the master of the harvest to send out laborers for his harvest."

Reflection:

How am I currently working for God's harvest?

What more can I do as a laborer for the harvest?

What prevents me from being a laborer?

In our world today, I see a hunger for the truth. I see this in people of all ages and from all backgrounds. The harvest is truly overflowing, and the laborers are few. The harvest is happening at this moment in our homes, at work, at school, at stores, at amusement parks, on subways, and on our computers. Being a laborer can take many forms, such as being a blogger, a passenger on a plane, a co-worker, a teacher, a customer, a student, or having an online social media profile, but each of these forms has a common thread...they are witnesses to the love and grace of God.

Lesson 9:

Various points along the Camino had kilometer markers letting travelers know the distance to Santiago. Initially, eight hundred kilometers does not seem that far, but after walking a couple of days in the mountains, it's easy to realize how far the distance is. A sign in one town was publicizing its winery to pilgrims. It said that the distance to Santiago was only 576 kilometers away, and I realized that my Camino pilgrimage was already a quarter over. What had initially seemed so far away was getting closer to being over.

That reminded me of my twenty-fifth birthday. I had realized that if I lived to be one hundred, I had already spent 25 percent of my life. For some reason, twenty-five was a hard birthday for me because, although I had achieved success by society's standards by that age, I still felt I had not lived my life to the fullest.

To bring the point home about enjoying every moment of the Camino experience, that evening I had dinner with a woman from Holland. Holland had a special twinkle in her eye, and over dinner, as we shared who we were and why we walked, I understood where she got her twinkle. She had a diagnosis of cancer and was given six months to live. She had received the diagnosis three years prior. She chose to live her life fully instead of waiting for death to overtake her. Holland needed to walk at a slower pace, and she jokingly referred to it as the "Camino lite," but she was still enjoying the time she had left and was living her life.

Often we get frustrated with our lives and the cards we are dealt, and we fail to realize the joy of situations or the experiences we are in. We rush to finish our workweeks so we can enjoy weekends, and we fail to appreciate the weeks we have been given and everything that goes along with them.

Scripture Meditation: Isaiah 41:10

Fear not, I am with you; be not dismayed; I am your God. I will strengthen you, and help you, and uphold you with my right hand of justice.

Reflection:

When in my life do I wish I had slowed down to enjoy and appreciate that time more?

How can I live more in the moment in my daily life?

We can think about the past, we can plan for our futures, but we can never stop living in the moment. The moments we live in right now will determine our futures. In this moment, God has given a gift. Our job is to realize the gift we have been given at this very moment and to enjoy the beauty that surrounds us, from the people we meet to the ordinary tasks of our daily lives. For when we do ordinary tasks with great love, they become extraordinary.

Lesson 10:

Two brothers I met at the beginning of my journey were also walking the Camino de Santiago for religious discernment. They told me they planned to take Sundays off to allow for a day of rest. I thought this sounded like an excellent plan, so I tried to coordinate my time to spend Sundays in towns with a convent so that I could participate in morning lauds, adoration, evening vespers, and night compline, as well as attend Mass. The Camino is meant to keep pilgrims walking toward Santiago, so hikers cannot stay for more than one night at most places unless they are sick or injured. So, I would often try to stay in a town on Saturday evening that was five kilometers or so away from a town I desired to spend Sunday in. That allowed me to wake up, walk, and arrive for morning lauds at the convent. There was only one Sunday when I had to walk about twenty kilometers to arrive in a town that had a convent.

I left Cicero, Spain, in pitch-blackness, and I arrived in Santo Domingo just as morning lauds were taking place. After morning lauds, I had breakfast at a café and then returned to the chapel of the Cistercian nuns to pray and attend Mass. After Mass, I was able to check in at the Cistercian nun's monastery, and they gave the option to stay more than one day. Had I previously known that, I would have spent Saturday and Sunday evening with them instead of the place in Cicero. As a side note, the place in Cicero was the only place that felt a bit scary to me (like horror-movie scary), but it was also the place where I was able to have the amazing conversation with the young German fellow.

So, after Mass and washing my laundry (this town also offered a washing and drying machine), I returned to the chapel to pray. Evening vespers and adoration took place together, and they were incredible. In that chapel, God spoke to me through His word. I sat in the chapel on the front pew, and I was praying and offering up my pain to God. During adoration, I read Luke 12, and it hit me—I just had to laugh at myself. Part of my Camino experience included me being humbled. I have always had a healthy self-confidence (sometimes to a fault), and there I was physically in pain and walking slower than most other people were. I had shared with fellow pilgrims that, back home, others considered me to be in good shape. After ten years of working, I could still out kayak my students when we raced (but it had gotten harder each year). I could play sports all night long at a lock-in with teenagers at my church. And just four months prior in New York, I was walking fourteen hours a day, carrying my student's backpacks full of souvenirs for them. But on the Camino, I was beat! My legs wanted to give way, and at night in the albergue, they did. My back felt the pain, and my feet were constantly getting sympathy from fellow pilgrims. Yet, part of my Camino experience and blessing was the humbling. I was not the fastest; others passed me. I was not able to carry other pilgrims' bags, and I had accepted that. Now, when you read Luke 12, you might wonder from where I got the humbling concept. Well, Luke 12 is the story of a man who stored up treasure to rest and take it easy, but on that night he died (can we say Kim's life plan?). A later passage follows with, "To whom much is given, much will be required." You see, I know I am blessed, and only through God's grace have I lived the life I have led and have the gifts that I have. I have done nothing to deserve them, nor will I ever be able to do anything to deserve them. That is why they are gifts—we do not earn gifts but receive gifts.

Humbling ourselves is not a bad thing. Although, in our society, when others humble us, it appears as if they have beaten us, and being humbled appears as a negative. Truth is, when we are humbled, we are better students. Living in our own arrogance, we can forget that everything comes from God and everything belongs to Him. We end up living life like the rich man who stored up treasure, instead of living like Job, who knew God gave him all his wealth and that God could reclaim it at any time.

A humbling moment I have come to appreciate is my speech problem. I spent six years in speech therapy, and there are still sounds I cannot hear properly, which means I do not say them properly. Whenever I give a keynote speech or host a retreat, I am mindful to avoid those words. As a speaker, I am able to connect to an audience, and through storytelling, I can keep them entertained while I teach. Every speaker will tell you he or she loves to see a crowd on fire for the information—to see people wanting to make changes to their lives. When I speak, passion fills me, and I might be on fire, but all it takes is one mistake and one person in the audience to comment on an error in my speech to humble me. This might be frustrating for some, but in all honesty, I view this humbling as a gift when I am speaking. It helps keep my ego and me in balance.

In the same way, as I sat in the Cistercian nun's chapel, I was humbled, and that helped me to grow spiritually. For although I was humbled, I also was given reassurance by God that He wanted me to use the gifts He had given me.

Scripture Meditation: Luke 12:16-23; 27-28; 49

Then he told them a parable. "There was a rich man whose land produced a bountiful harvest. He asked himself, 'What shall I do, for I do not have space to store my harvest?' And he said, 'This is what I shall do: I shall tear down my barns and build larger ones. There I shall store all my grain and other goods and I shall say to myself, "Now as for you, you have stored up for many years, rest, eat, drink, be merry!"' But God said to him, 'You fool, this very night your life will be demanded of you; and the things you have prepared, to whom will they belong?' Thus will it be for the one who stores up treasure for himself but is not rich in what matters to God." He said to [his] disciples, "Therefore I tell you, do not worry about your life and what you will eat, or about your body and what you will wear. For life is more than food and the body more than clothing."

"Notice how the flowers grow. They do not toil or spin. But I tell you, not even Solomon in all splendor was dressed like one of them. If God

so clothes the grass in the field that grows today and is thrown into the oven tomorrow, will he not much more provide for you, O you of little faith?"

"I have come to set the earth on fire, and how I wish it were already blazing!"

Reflection:

Do I take for granted all that I have? Do I acknowledge and truly believe that everything I have is from God?

In what ways have I been humbled in my life? How did I take being humbled?

Do I accept God humbling me so that He can use me in greater ways?

I left the chapel and returned to the bunkhouse, where I prayed and gave thanks to God for sharing His word with me. I even shared the story with my bunkmates that evening. On the following day's walk, I thought about my prayer time in the chapel. As fellow pilgrims continued to pass me by, I reflected on being humbled and using that to grow spiritually. The teacher, to make sure this student learned the lesson, sent me a visual aid I will never forget: a blind man holding the arm of a fellow pilgrim passing me. I was truly amazed and thought it hammered home the point God was making. By the time I was able to get my camera out of my pocket and up to take the photo, the men were out of sight. God has a sense of humor!

Lesson 11:

From my very first day walking the Camino, I chose to thank God for the blessings He gave me. There were many blessings, and each day the weather gave me a chance to give thanks for them. The weather was constantly changing, and I went from walking in the heat, wearing my shorts and shirt, to wearing my winter coat and still feeling cold in the harsh wind. Yet, in the extreme wind, heat, rain, or cold, I was able to find and give thanks to God for His blessing. For after walking a few days in heat, I would thank God for rain clouds, which would cool things down. And in the extreme cold, I found it easy to give God thanks, because the cold numbed the pain in my legs and feet. In the same way, when it rained, I thanked God for cooling me down and reminding me of my Baptismal promise.

Many of us are guilty of seeing a glass half empty instead of half full. When it rains on a weekend, we complain that we cannot go to the lake instead of thanking God for filling the lake with water. I know, it is hard to always view things with a positive attitude, but it is actually harder to always view things with a negative attitude. Negative attitudes hinder us both mentally and physically. Whereas, when we have positive attitudes, our mental and physical lives actually improve. When I worked at a college, I always trained my staff on the FISH! Philosophy, which had four principles. To me the most important one was "choose your attitude." The thought process is simple: we cannot choose everything that will happen today. Regardless of what a supervisor does, what homework a teacher assigns, if we get in accidents, or if we receive bad news, we can always choose our attitudes about these situations.

When I was in college, bad drivers who cut me off would extremely irritate me. Now, I was not to the point of using profanity, but it did anger me. Then one day I realized that a person who cuts me off moves on with his or her day, while I get upset and sometimes start my day with anger. That is when I made a conscious decision to begin praying for that person to be a safe driver and for God to protect him or her. Instead of getting angry, that shift in my attitude had a positive result on both my mental and physical self. Ever notice people who get angry when they drive? Their hands wave inappropriately, or they tighten their grips on the steering wheels. I guarantee those actions get to their hearts. Scientists tell us that people who are more prone to get angry have a higher risk for heart disease than people who remain calm.

Then there is also the ripple effect; our attitudes will affect the attitudes of the people around us. If you go to work with a bad attitude and complain, people will either join in with you or pull away from you. In college, I was a resident assistant (RA) and loved my job, and the bad parts of the job always lent themselves to funny stories later on, so they did not bother me. I would take the bad times in stride and keep a positive outlook. Well, one of my fellow

RAs often complained about the job and criticized me for loving the job so much. So one day, I simply told her that she should quit. I did not want to be around her and her negative attitude because I really liked my job. I clearly remember the staff member taking a step back, but then I began to notice a change in her attitude for the better.

So remember, each day we can choose our attitudes and how we will respond. Part of our responses to God need to be giving Him thanks and acknowledging the blessings He gives us. Look around your own life and count all the blessings God has given you. If I were to sit down with a pen and paper and record the blessings in my life, I would fill a journal, and I am sure you would too. So, even when something might not look like a blessing, I challenge you to find the blessing in disguise!

Scripture Meditation: Psalm 100

A psalm of thanksgiving. Shout joyfully to the LORD, all you lands; worship the LORD with cries of gladness; come before him with joyful song. Know that the LORD is God, our maker to whom we belong, whose people we are, God's well-tended flock. Enter the temple gates with praise, its courts with thanksgiving. Give thanks to God, bless his name; good indeed is the LORD, Whose love endures forever, whose faithfulness lasts through every age.

Reflection:

How often in my day do I give thanks to God?

How do I give thanks for the conversations, people, places, gifts, and things in my life?

What is one thing that always upsets me, and how can I change how I view it?

The practice of giving thanks for the blessings God has given us is something we have to work on. In our society, we often find ourselves competing with others that we fail to recognize all the blessings we have. Often, missionaries who serve in third-world countries return shell-shocked by the excesses of our culture. We often fail to recognize the abundance we have in our desperate attempt to get more. Take time today and every day to thank God for the blessings in your life, even when they might not seem like blessings. Put on your positive attitude to find the blessings hidden in every cloud.

Lesson 12:

One of the people I met was a pilgrim from the Netherlands, and it was his 101st day walking on the Camino. Like pilgrims of the medieval days, he began walking toward Santiago from his home. He was not the only European pilgrim I met who began walking from his home, but this is a rarity nowadays on the Camino. When we talked about why we each walked, he talked about the need to break his addiction. He had found himself trapped in pornography and video games, and he knew he needed a change. Trying to change at his home proved too difficult, as the temptations were all around him. So, he began his pilgrimage to Santiago and spent his time walking and reading the Bible.

What my friend from the Netherlands had figured out is something public speakers often teach when speaking to people about changing their lives. We often feel trapped in routines, and these routines become habit. Now, depending on what leadership speaker you listen to, you will hear it takes anywhere from twenty-eight to forty days to create a new habit. I have always been fond of forty days, since it has a biblical reference to it.

Change is hard. We are often creatures of habit, and when we are required to change for jobs, for relationships, or even for God, we find it challenging. To remove habits from our lives, we first become aware of them and have a true desire to change. Then we make conscious decisions and begin uprooting those habits from our lives. We often will remove temptations that lead us to habits, which can be things or people. Then, it is also helpful to replace a bad habit with a new, positive habit. That way, when we have the desire to go to the old, bad habits, we recognize the need and then shift our attention to the new habits.

By walking the Camino, he removed the easy access he had to his laptop back home, which had allowed him to view pornography. He chose to go on a spiritual pilgrimage, which would limit his exposure to sexual images on the Internet, as well as on television shows. He also realized he spent a lot of unproductive time playing video games, so he removed himself from having access to video games as well. To replace the time he had previously spent doing those activities, he began walking about twelve hours a day. Then when his body was physically exhausted, he would stop walking, find a place to stay for lodging, and read the Bible. What I love about him choosing to begin reading the Bible (for he was previously not a religious man) is the fact that he found comfort and strength through the words of our Lord. When we seek to truly change our lives and bad habits, there is nothing greater than turning to God and asking for His assistance.

All Christians would agree that pornography in any amount is evil, and a person should earnestly strive to remove that addiction from his or her life. But the habit of playing video games is not as clear. The key thing to consider is not that all video games are evil, but that if we spend too much time playing them, we waste the life God has given us.

Scripture Meditation: Mark 9:42-48

"Whoever causes one of these little ones who believe [in me] to sin, it would be better for him if a great millstone were put around his neck and he were thrown into the sea. If your hand causes you to sin, cut it off. It is better for you to enter into life maimed than with two hands to go into Gehenna, into the unquenchable fire. And if your foot causes you to sin, cut it off. It is better for you to enter into life crippled than with two feet to be thrown into Gehenna. And if your eye causes you to sin, pluck it out. Better for you to enter into the kingdom of God with one eye than with two eyes to be thrown into Gehenna, where 'their worm does not die, and the fire is not quenched.

Reflection:

Is there a place, thing, or person in my life that is causing me to have a bad habit?

What am I willing to do to get rid of that habit?

What is a new, positive habit I want in my life and how can I implement it?

For only Christ is perfect; the rest of us strive to imitate Christ, and this is why we each need to create positive habits that can replace negative habits. We are a creation by God, and just like our physical bodies, our interior bodies and our spirituality are constantly changing shape. Make sure that you spend more time working on habits that impact your soul as opposed to habits that impact your physical image. People go to great lengths to get in shape but rarely make the same effort to get their souls in shape. The majority of people spend more time at gyms and beauty parlors or selecting wardrobes than reading the Bible or praying. Genesis 3:19 tells us, "*For you are dust, and to dust you shall return.*" Our physical bodies will be buried and decay in the ground, while our spiritual souls are made for an eternity.

Lesson 13:

After a very long day of hiking, I arrived in a small town where a couple had opened their home to pilgrims. They have one bedroom that accommodates eight pilgrims. Michelle and Felix have a passion for the Camino, and the Camino is their life and ministry. Michelle is French, and Felix is Spanish. They met some years back while they each hiked the Camino. As I sat in their foyer while Michelle recorded my information, I looked around the walls at all their Camino trinkets and their compostela certificates. Felix is the storyteller out of the two, and although he could not really speak English, he was so animated when he spoke in Spanish that I could understand a good amount of what he shared. Together the two have hiked the Camino either by themselves or together twenty-six times. They are religious pilgrims who see the Camino as a religious experience, and strive to share the true meaning of the Camino with fellow pilgrims.

When it came time for dinner, we all gathered around their kitchen table, and Michelle gave a greeting and beautiful blessing, making us feel like guests instead of visitors. In addition, Michelle knew that I did not like eggs, so she prepared a special dinner for me, because the main dish was eggs for the other pilgrims. Following dinner, Felix told some Camino stories, we sang Spanish songs, and then it was time for bed. Michelle asked me to come to the foyer so she could look at my feet, because she had noticed my limp. My feet were severely cracked with blisters, but the blister on the bottom pad of my foot caused the worst pain. I sat in a chair, and Michelle sat across from me. She took my feet in her hands, washed them, and examined my method of treatment. For the blisters, I had used the needle and thread technique to slowly drain them but was afraid of infection, so I was constantly replacing the thread. Michelle told me my thread was too small, so she replaced the thread, tied big loops with the thread, put on a special disinfectant to dry out the blisters, and then used toilet paper to create padding for my foot.

It was while this complete stranger was tenderly treating my foot that I understood in my heart, for the first time, the true act of compassion that Veronica offered our Lord on His way to Calvary, and how we are each called to love our neighbor as if we are loving Christ. There a complete stranger saw my pain and cared for me as if I were Christ. There was nothing in it for Michelle. The reality is we will most likely never meet again, yet she shared Christ's love for me. In my life, I have stopped and helped many people. I have always been a service Christian, but I wonder if I have ever had true compassion—the compassion that Michelle gave me. Have I ever helped someone and made that person feel the love as if I were helping Jesus Christ?

To Michelle it might have been a simple act, seeing a pilgrim in pain and offering compassionate relief, but for me it was the greatest act of love a stranger has ever given me. The next morning after breakfast, I hugged Michelle and Felix goodbye, put on my backpack, and walked out of their home. It was dark, and they followed me to the door and stood in the street waving goodbye. It was as if they were my own parents waving goodbye to me, and I even got a little choked up. I wanted to always remember them, so I took a picture, but because it was dark outside, the photo did not take. As I write this chapter, I still can see Felix standing there with his hands raised in the air, telling a story. And I see Michelle sitting there in a chair with my feet in her lap.

Scripture Meditation: Matthew 25:34-40

"Then the king will say to those on his right, 'Come, you who are blessed by my Father. Inherit the kingdom prepared for you from the foundation of the world. For I was hungry and you gave me food, I was thirsty and you gave me drink, a stranger and you welcomed me, naked and you clothed me, ill and you cared for me, in prison and you visited me.' Then the righteous will answer him and say, 'Lord, when did we see you hungry and feed you, or thirsty and give you drink? When did we see you a stranger and welcome you, or naked and clothe you? When did we see you ill or in prison, and visit you?' And the king will say to them in reply, 'Amen, I say to you, whatever you did for one of these least brothers of mine, you did for me.'"

Reflection:

When has someone served me as if he or she were serving Jesus?

How can I show compassion to others in my daily life?

As a Christian, I struggle to see Jesus Christ in everyone I meet, but I know this is what God calls us to do as Christians. Theologically, I know every person is made in the image and likeness of God, but I still have a hard time connecting my heart to my brain. I ask for your prayers that I may be a better disciple of Jesus Christ and serve everyone as if I am serving Jesus himself. My prayers are also with each of you reading this book. If you struggle in this area as well, may you, too, come to see Jesus Christ in all you serve.

Lesson 14:

Michelle recommended certain places along the Camino that hold historical importance, and she encouraged us to live the authentic pilgrim experience. She told us we would come across San Anton ruins that for hundreds of years had hosted a church, convent, and hospital, which had taken care of pilgrims. Though the buildings are in ruins, pilgrims can still spend the night, which gives an authentic experience, even though there is no electricity or hot water. Although I was fond of Michelle, I had planned to not stay there, because I wanted electricity and a hot shower. However, in the distance, I saw the massive ruins of an old church, and I got excited to explore the site that is out in the middle of nowhere. As I entered the grounds to look at them, I realized they were San Anton, and I knew that was where I wanted to spend the night.

The sidewalls of the structure are all that remain from the original structure, and inside the church walls is a small shelter for pilgrims. I entered the doors and gave my standard Spanish greeting, "Buenos Tardes, Senor!" To which the gentleman responded in very fast Spanish. He quickly understood that I did not speak Spanish fluently, and I understood that he did not speak English. I was waiting for him to stamp my credentials and show me to the bed, but he seemed hesitant as he continued eating his lunch. I then said, "Michelle y Felix recommendo," to which he amazingly understood. He repeated their names and became very hospitable, inviting me to sit down and asking if I wanted some soup or his kiwi. He then got up and showed me to my bed. We tried to communicate in Spanish, and then he left.

About an hour later, a couple from England I had met on and off, since my second day, arrived to look at the ruins. Upon entering, they saw me sitting at the table by myself. They asked if anyone was there, and I told them what I thought the man had told me (if I understood his Spanish).

"He left to take a nap. If others come, I am to show them to their beds. Dinner is at 7:00 p.m. He is either coming back to cook, or I am cooking dinner. And I am in charge as the hospitalero."

The couple knew my Spanish was lacking, but it seemed like too good of an adventure to pass up, so the couple decided to stay. We tried very hard to market the San Anton ruins to fellow pilgrims who came by, and some were very interested, since the place had almost a thousand-year history, but whenever we mentioned no electricity and no hot water, they left.

We got our beds ready, as we knew it would be getting dark soon. And we decided to skip the cold shower because it was so cold. We sat around the table as the night approached, drinking hot tea. Before 7:00 p.m., the man returned and seemed surprised that there were three of us. The woman could speak Spanish, so she communicated back and forth with the man for the rest of the evening, translating for her boyfriend and me. We all helped prepare dinner, and after dinner, we lit the lanterns, and the man played the guitar. It was time for bed, so the man left and told us he would lock us in. But, he wanted us to wait for his return in the morning so that the buildings would be secure.

This story, I think, sums up responding to God's will. I spend a lot of time in prayer, asking God what His will is, as well as asking for the knowledge to know His will and the strength to do His will. Yet, I have never heard God's voice come down to me. Usually, I feel a nudge inside my innermost being, or every now and then, a word or phrase comes to me from that same place. Sometimes, I am unsure where a nudge is leading me, but I trust God and have faith in Him to have the Holy Spirit guide me, and I begin doing what I think He is leading me to do. In the same way, I was not sure what the man had told me before he left, but I began doing what I thought he had told me and began greeting pilgrims to the place. Upon his return (through our translator), we learned that what I had heard was accurate. In the same way, God guides us through the Holy Spirit, and if we get off course, He nudges us to get back on course. In addition, just as I had a translator, sometimes God chooses to use translators for our spiritual lives and sends people to say something to us that we immediately recognize as the truth from God.

Scripture Meditation: John 21:4-7

When it was already dawn, Jesus was standing on the shore; but the disciples did not realize that is was Jesus. Jesus said to them, "Children, have you caught anything to eat?" They answered him, "No." So he said to them, "Cast the net over to the right side of the boat and you will find something." So they cast it, and were not able to pull it in because of the number of fish. So the disciple whom Jesus loved said to Peter, "It is the Lord."

Reflection:

When was a time that God used a translator in my life to show me the truth?

Do I listen and then act on the direction God is leading me in? When have I not listened?

When was a time that I was pleasantly surprised after following God's will?

Although it was the coldest night on the Camino, it was my best night of sleep. The three of us used all the blankets from the other beds, as there were no other pilgrims with us. The thick blankets were military-style, and the six I had covered me from head to toe. The weight of the blankets literally caused me to struggle to turn in my bed. But between the three of us, we had a snore-free night (a Camino first), and I remained warm and slept through the entire night (another Camino first). So, by deciding to stay at the place all other pilgrims passed up, I had the best night's sleep, just like when we choose God's will over ours, we find peace.

Lesson 15:

I always knew that living in the United States was a blessing and that I took many things for granted, like the typical American. In our culture what we consider the poverty level is what many parts of the world consider being rich. I also know that I was blessed to have grown up in the home that I did, and that I have never been hungry from a lack of food. But during my time on the Camino, I came to appreciate all that I have. Going from two thousand square feet of stuff in my home to a twenty-seven-pound backpack of stuff was a dramatic shift. For the most part, I passed through small towns on the Camino, realizing all the things that I took for granted that these rural communities did not have. On the trip, as I realized what these towns did not have, I began realizing how much of life I took for granted and never thanked God for the things that seemed normal to me. And the amazing thing was that I did not miss those things I had previously taken for granted. Instead, I thanked God for what He did provide me. My attitude was "the glass is half full," and I thanked God for giving me that much water to drink.

The things I had previously taken for granted were many: air conditioning, heating, screens on windows, bathtubs, hot water, electricity, washing machines and dryers, toilets, toilet paper, Q-tips, American hamburgers, Dr. Pepper, clean tap water, bath gel, more than two pairs of socks, and so many more conveniences. These were all things that I had never even thought about. Each time I turned on the lights at my house, I did not stop and marvel at that gift or give thanks to God in appreciation for that gift. No, I simply turned on the light (expecting it to be there) and went on about my day. But after staying at a place with no electricity, I realized the gift of that light switch.

On hot days, we slept with the windows open, because there was no air conditioning in any of the places that I stayed. Often, bugs would enter since the windows had no screens on them. On those hot days, I gave thanks for the weather, because at least my clothes would dry on the line overnight. When the weather turned cold, I noticed that the majority of places had no heat, and I wore every piece of clothing I had to keep from freezing at night. On the coldest nights, I found myself not being angry that the cold kept me awake but instead offered thanks to God that I was inside, even if the building was a bit drafty. Most towns did not have a washing machine, and even fewer had a dryer. It was a special day when I had my clothes cleaned in an actual washing machine (four times over the forty days). So, upon arrival at my albergue in the afternoons, I would shower and then immediately hand wash my clothes so they could begin drying. I only brought two pairs of each of my items, so it was important to have my clothes dry overnight; otherwise, the wet clothes would hang on my bag the following day as I hiked. So, each afternoon I stood at a sink and washed my clothes with soap and arm muscle. As I did this, I gave thanks to God that I had a sink and was not having to wash my clothes in a river.

Even though I had less on the Camino, it felt like I had so much more. With a joyful heart, I was grateful for what I did have, and I gave gratitude to God for what He provided. I know in certain Christian denominations, the prosperity message has become popular. So often, we want religion to conform to us instead of us conforming to religion, and that is when we begin changing religion from what God intended it to be. Personally, I do not believe in the prosperity message that God wants me to be rich, and that if I am faithful to God, He will take care of me financially. If we look to Jesus and the church that He began with His apostles, we see that He never promised them riches in this world. On the complete contrary, many gave up their fortunes to serve Him. In addition, His people did not lead glamorous lives as the kings did. They were mistreated, and every apostle was killed, with the exception of John (though they tried to kill John). Yet we know the apostles were happy; they died joyfully, from the first martyr, Saint Stephen, until the most recent martyrs. These holy men and women have complete trust that the Good Shepherd will provide for them spiritually and bring them into His eternal kingdom. They had gratitude for all that the Lord had done for them and gave thanks that they could die a martyr for our Lord.

On the Camino, I gave thanks for everything. Having less made me more grateful for the abundance I had before but also for the few things I have now. It made me connect to all the people of this world that go without clean water, hot showers, and electricity. Even though each of these minor inconveniences was only temporary for me, it made me appreciate what I did have.

Scripture Meditation: 1 Thessalonians 5:16-18

Rejoice always. Pray without ceasing. In all circumstances give thanks, for this is the will of God for you in Christ Jesus.

Reflection:

How often do I thank God for the many blessings He has given me?

When am I more likely to tell God my gratitude for His many gifts?

When am I least likely to tell God my gratitude for His many gifts? What can I find to be thankful for right now?

When we begin following Jesus, the Jesus of the Bible, we are able to see joy in everything, and we constantly want to sing praises to our Lord. What in your day have you used that you have taken for granted? Nothing that I have is my own. God gives me everything, and He can take everything away, for I am a steward of the Lord. When I begin with the thought that nothing is mine, I become grateful for what God loans to me. If your car has ever broken down, and a friend loaned you his or her car, you understand the appreciation you have for the car. Guess what? God is that friend, and He has loaned you everything in your life!

Lesson 16:

One of the many blessings of the Camino was all the people I met and how I formed a family among the pilgrims. Everyone on the Camino moved at his or her own pace, and I never knew when would be the last time I would come across a certain pilgrim again. Once I started taking Sundays off and walking slower due to my injuries, I quit seeing the same people each night at the albergues or at dinner. At first, I did notice that I missed those people. After all, they were people I had my first Camino experiences with. But through that separation, I did find my relationship with God had deepened, and I met so many other pilgrims I would have never met had I stayed with the same people the entire time.

But, just like at a family reunion, I love reuniting with family members I have lost touch with, and the same is true on the Camino. After walking for about ten days without running into any of the other pilgrims I had met on the early part of my journey, I was completely surprised one morning after topping a steep incline up a mountain to run into "the mother."

The mother was hiking with her two adult daughters, and I had met each one of them separately during the first two days of my journey. All three women were outgoing and very easy to talk with. I had shared a brief conversation with the oldest daughter on my first day in Orission, France, where we had taken shelter from the rain and enjoyed a hot drink, since the morning had been wet and cold. That evening at the albergue, I had a conversation over the shower wall with her younger sister and, ironically, on the following night, we once again would talk over the shower wall before we ever met face to face. Then on the second evening, I sat in the yard of our albergue and talked with the mother. I saw the three of them off and on again over the first few days but do not recall seeing them again after Pamplona.

So, you can imagine my surprise when many days later, I ran into them upon arriving at the top of the mountain. For the rest of that day, I would rotate between one of the three, and we would have conversations covering the spectrum of life. It happened to be the birthday of the younger sister, and they invited me to join them for her birthday dinner. After arriving in town and settling down, I went looking for the church (so often the time of the pilgrim menu and the Mass conflicted). I felt my heart divided, as it was nice to run into familiar friends again. For the previous two weeks, my injury had caused me to not walk as far each day, which meant that I rarely saw the same pilgrims two days in a row, so all my relationships had been short-term. But here I had the chance to share a meal and an evening of laughs with friends.

As I went to Mass, I thought it was funny that, even on a spiritual pilgrimage, I could find my heart divided between worldly pleasures and heavenly pleasures. One thing I have come to know is that attending Mass and being nourished by Jesus is more fulfilling and lasting than anything else I have ever known, yet I still felt the temptation.

Scripture Meditation: 1 Corinthians 10:13

No trial has come to you but what is human. God is faithful and will not let you be tried beyond your strength; but with the trial he will also provide a way out, so that you may be able to bear it.

Reflection:

Have I ever felt an internal pull between worldly and heavenly pleasures? What did I choose?

When have I felt I was being tested beyond my limits, but God gave me strength to overcome? How did I feel after overcoming the trial?

I do not think our lives are made on big decisions but on the little decisions we make every minute of every day. Yes, big decisions can impact our lives drastically, but those big decisions usually come after many smaller decisions have helped shape them. Walking away from my director position at the college, after being there ten years, to trust God and discover His will for my life was a big decision with big impacts. But before I ever made that decision, I made hundreds of smaller decisions. I take comfort in the Bible verse above, because I know God will never give me more than I can handle, and He always gives me the grace I need for the test at hand.

Lesson 17:

In Carrion de los Condes, while staying at the Monastery of Santa Clara, I was blessed with being there on a Sunday to participate in Adoration, as well as Liturgy of the Hours. The nuns, after singing night vespers, became very quiet, simply focusing on Jesus in the Eucharist. In the stillness and silence of that church, I went to the Bible to hear the words God had chosen for me.

As I read my Bible, the verse, "*he must increase, I must decrease,*" really came to me. My very first thought was, "How can He increase and I decrease?" I know I talk a lot, many of my conversations are about me, and I utilize stories to draw people in, but that puts so much focus on me. I began reflecting on how I could turn all my conversations to God. How I could truly allow Him to increase inside of me and allow myself to decrease. Part of this also led me to realize that I have to let Christ's goodness shine from me.

Scripture Meditation: John 3:30

"He must increase; I must decrease."

Reflection:

In what ways must I decrease to allow Christ to increase in my life?

How can I allow Christ's light to shine forth from me?

Knowing that anything good within me comes from God creates a desire within me to allow God to be ever more present in my life, my words, and my actions. Allowing God to increase in my life will allow me to become the person God intended me to be.

Lesson 18

Many people walk the Camino with companions. Usually they have arrived together, but sometimes on the trail, they meet someone or a group, and they walk about the same distance each day and begin walking together. Some groups were even walking the Camino together, such as the church from Italy that had about thirty pilgrims in its group or the Spanish family of twelve (three generations) walking together. I saw friends walking together, as well as mother/daughter, father/son, grandmother/granddaughter, and brother / sister combinations. But my favorite was when I saw married couples walking together.

The entire context of marriage is that a husband and wife will grow closer together, as well as closer to God in their relationship. One evening at the albergue, I had dinner with a newlywed, German couple walking the Camino for their honeymoon. They were full of faith, and the Camino had always been something the husband had wanted to do. The wife knew it was her husband's dream, so it had become her dream as well. The husband knew everything about the Camino. He had memorized every town and the distance between towns. They loved walking the Camino, but they also wanted to acknowledge that the experience was their honeymoon. So, they had decided to stay in private rooms instead of the bunkhouses as much as possible. In addition, the husband carried the supplies, while his wife only had a small pack to carry.

The Camino experience gave that husband and wife an opportunity that many couples will never be able to experience—the gift of their total selves and their time. Nowadays, we have so many distractions that we fail to be truly present to our spouses. In the same way, we allow distractions and noise to keep us from God. Noise and distractions also keep us from the people that matter the most. Our culture has had an increase in children being born outside of marriage, as well as an increase in divorce, because as a society, we have failed to give the gift of total self and our time. If you were to give the gift of total self, then that would include marriage before sex, which would reduce the number of children being born to single mothers. If you were to give the gift of time, then you would grow with the person you married instead of growing apart, which would reduce the number of divorces. We all have a past, and somewhere along the way, we have each fallen short from the lives God has called us to live. There is hope; we have a loving God—a God who sent His only Son to die for us, so that we might be forgiven and be reunited with Him forever. Begin today by making God the center of your life, and if you are married, the center of your marriage.

Scripture Meditation: Genesis 2: 24

That is why a man leaves his father and mother and clings to his wife, and the two of them become one body.

Reflection:

In my marriage, do I give my total self without allowing distractions to take my attention from my spouse? If not married, how would I plan to not allow distraction to take my attention from my spouse?

Does God have a place in my relationships with other people?

If married, in what ways can I allow God to be the focus of my marriage? If not married, how can I allow God to be the focus of my life?

I am not married, but I do not have to be married to know that marriage takes effort. This young couple gave their total selves to one another and made a pilgrimage together so they could grow closer together and closer to God. I also met a beautiful older Spanish couple on the trail, who were holding hands. With their free hands, they used walking sticks. Whether you are married or not, the lesson remains that you need to give your total self in your relationships, and make sure God is a part of every relationship you have.

Lesson 19:

One day as I arrived in a town, I began looking for the Benedictine Monastery to spend the night. I stopped a gentleman on the street to ask for directions. He responded in Spanish, and I understood the general direction he was sending me. Before we parted, he pulled out a Saint James keychain and told me he had hiked to Santiago before. Then he asked me to pray for him and his eye when I arrived in Santiago. He pointed at his almost-closed eye, and I could see it had an infection. I told the man I would pray for him, and we departed.

As I walked and prayed for the gentleman, I thought about the gift of relief we so often give the people in our lives through our prayers. But we know that our prayers are not limited to those who surround us on this earth.

As Christians, we believe that after this life, we will spend our eternities in heaven or hell, and that our spiritual lives will carry on forever. Yes, our bodies will decay and return to the dust, which God created us from, but our souls are meant to last forever. Because we believe in this afterlife, we are not bound by prayers of those we can physically see. We can also ask for prayers from those who have gone on before us. Our family members, our friends, and holy men and women of God who are in heaven are praying for us. The term intercessory prayer means we ask others to pray to God on our behalf. The gentleman did not pray to me asking me to heal him; he asked me to pray to God for him. In the same way, I ask those in heaven to pray for me. When we request prayers from our family or friends, we often go to those people who appear to have a close relationship with God. Have you ever gone to a bar as it was closing and looked for a drunk and stumbling person to ask for prayers? No, I bet you have gone to church and seen someone praying and then gone to him or her to ask for prayers for you or a family member. The same is true about those in heaven; we seek prayers from those who have a close relationship with God. Many of these holy men and women have been named saints for their lifestyles, but of course, there are many holy men and women in heaven who are not called saints. But I still ask for their prayers.

One of the big misconceptions about Catholics is that we pray to saints. People see the statues, prayer cards, and relics of these Saints in the Catholic Churches and in the homes of practicing Catholics, and they automatically call it idol worship. Well, if having an image of someone you love, respect, and look up to is considered idol worship, I challenge you to enter a home in America and not find pictures of family members and friends. Why do people have pictures of family on nightstands? Why is a child's artwork on a refrigerator? People save photos and a child's first tooth because they love that person, want to keep him or her close, and remember important moments. The same is true of the images we see of Saints—we love them, want to keep them close, and remember important moments of their lives.

In our earthly relationships, we are attracted to certain people based on their characteristics. In the same way, we are attracted to Saints in heaven based on their characteristics. As earthly friends have comforted me when I have had a rough time, in the same way, my heavenly friends have offered me comfort. My pilgrimage originally was just going to consist of going to Lisieux to walk in the footsteps of Saint Therese, the Little Flower. Quickly the pilgrimage expanded to traveling through three countries and visiting many religious sites, which included the following Saints: Catherine Laboure of the Miraculous Medal, Mary (the mother of Jesus), Therese of Lisieux, Michael the Archangel, Bernadette of Lourdes, James the Apostle, Saint Theresa of Avila, and Saint John of the Cross. In addition, I visited many holy sites where apparitions had occurred, saw relics from the Lord's passion, and saw many more relics belonging to Saints not named. I went on a religious pilgrimage to see about my brothers and sisters who came before me, in the exact same way that I have been to the houses where my family members had lived in before I was ever born. When my great-granny passed away, my family traveled from Indiana to West Virginia to bury her. Upon arrival in West Virginia, we traveled to the small town and the site of her former house by the railroad tracks. We walked around the area, and we even took home with us an old rusty railroad nail, because my great-grandfather had worked on the railroad track. This was part of our family's history, and in the same way, I brought back a rose petal from the Carmel convent of Lisieux, a rock from the Camino, and a piece of Saint Theresa of Avila's clothing, provided by the nuns. These are things, just like my photos, that I can always remember my trip by, and they remind me of God. The rose petal reminds me of Therese's spirituality, where she encouraged us by doing small acts of love. The rock reminds me that I will often face stumbling blocks that I can turn into stepping-stones. Saint James death, along with the other apostles, was a stumbling block for them, but for the Christian faith, it was a stepping-stone. Their martyrdoms led many to the faith. Finally, the piece of clothing reminds me of Saint Theresa's determination to do God's will and not let anyone get in her way.

Scripture Meditation: Exodus 3:6

I am the God of your father, he continued, the God of Abraham, the God of Isaac, and the God of Jacob.

Scripture Meditation: Luke 20:34-38

Jesus said to them, "The children of this age marry and are given in marriage; but those who are deemed worthy to attain to the coming age and to the resurrection of the dead neither marry nor are given in marriage. They can no longer die, for they are like angels; and they are the children of God because they are the ones who will rise. That the dead will rise even Moses made known in the passage about the bush, when he called 'Lord' the God of Abraham, the God of Isaac,

*and the God of Jacob; and he is not God of the dead, but of the
living, for to him all are alive."*

Scripture Meditation: John 11:24-27

*Martha said to him, "I know he will rise, in the resurrection on the
last day." Jesus told her, "I am the resurrection and the life; whoever
believes in me, even if he dies, will live, and everyone who lives and
believes in me will never die. Do you believe this?" She said to him,
"Yes, Lord. I have come to believe that you are the Messiah, the Son
of God, the one who is coming into the world."*

Reflection:

Do I ask for intercessory prayers from those on earth or
those in heaven? Why?

Do I find it difficult to ask for prayers from those in
heaven or on earth?

What stops me from asking others to pray for me?

Jesus clearly tells us that when we die here on this earth,
we are alive with Him. When God talks to Moses, He does
not use past tense but present tense, which lets us know
He is still his God. In the Bible, the very first miracle
performed by Jesus happens after His mother goes to Him
as an intercessory for the bride and groom, who were out
of wine. The Saints did good while on earth for God's

kingdom. Why would they spend their heaven doing anything else? I think Saint Therese said it best. She died at the age of twenty-four and in her book, Story of a Soul she said, "When I die, I will send down a shower of roses from the heavens; I will spend my heaven by doing good on earth."

Lesson 20:

One thing I found funny on the Camino that also paralleled life was how many people skipped the middle section. From the start of my journey, over three hundred pilgrims spent the first night with me in Roncesvalles, Spain, and every day on the trail, I saw a good number of those pilgrims. Once I passed Pamplona, I noticed that fewer pilgrims were walking the trail, and some had planned to take a bus to Leon from Pamplona. There was still one more major decline of the pilgrims on the Camino and that was after I had passed through Burgos, Spain. Many pilgrims at Burgos took a bus to Leon. Many pilgrims took the bus because they said the landscape during the middle section was boring compared to walking in the mountains or through the vineyards. Some pilgrims would hike in and out of major cities then take a bus to the next big town.

One of the hospitaleros had told me that the Camino is broken into three sections. The first part is about physical challenge, the second part is about mental challenge, and the third part is about spiritual challenge. The middle section, with fewer pilgrims and less breathtaking scenery, challenges pilgrims the most. The distractions are all gone, and pilgrims only have themselves. For pilgrims traveling for fun and not religious reasons, this is when the Camino stops being fun and they take buses to Leon. Pilgrims skipping the middle section could potentially cheat their spiritual lives. Some people want to have the good without putting in any work. Many want testimonies without being tested. Some want mountaintop experiences with God but are not willing to climb a mountain. In our spiritual lives, it is the discipline we do out of love for God that helps us grow: spending time in prayer, meditating on the Bible, reading spiritual works, performing acts of mercy, and attending church. Yet, many people do not spend time with God on a regular basis. Instead, they only want Him around when they need something.

On the Camino, just like life, if people only want to do the fun parts, they will be around lots of people. But if they dive into their faith, they will find they desire time with God more than with people. In the middle section, many days I would hike the entire time by myself, and the only time I talked to fellow pilgrims was to say, "Buen Camino." But each evening I would gather with the church community and feel supported. In addition to the faith communities that God places in our lives, He gives us the best spiritual counselor, the Holy Spirit, to be with us always. Then, of course, there are the Angels and Saints in heaven who are supporting us and cheering for us as we choose our paths in life. So, whatever paths we choose, we are never alone. The question is, Do we take the easy path and catch that bus to the next big city, potentially missing out on what lessons God has for us? Or do we stay true to God's call and take the less popular path, where we learn from the teacher?

Scripture Meditation: Matthew 7:13-14

"Enter through the narrow gate; for the gate is wide and the road broad that leads to destruction, and those who enter through it are many. How narrow the gate and constricted the road that leads to life. And those who find it are few."

Reflection:

Have I created spiritual disciplines in my life to increase my time with God? How can I implement them daily?

What will I do to make sure I am not cheating on my spiritual life?

It is easy to be caught up in this world and get distracted. Distractions can prevent you from being the person God has called you to be. Imagine if Mary took a bus when the Angel came to her and told her she would have a child. How many people are missing their call from God because they are seeking a fun life? Yet the people who are living the life God has called them to seem to radiate a joy that those seeking fun are lacking. Jesus calls us to radical lives that are harder paths but offer more rewarding outcomes.

Lesson 21:

Many pilgrims, many cultures, many religions, many backgrounds, many values, and many conversations made me realize that I am not in the majority of this world. The values that so many of my peers on the Camino expressed were often conflicting with the values I held. In all these conversations, I realized that my beliefs stood as a stark contrast to the beliefs of the world today. Had I walked this Camino one hundred years before, I am confident my values would have been the same as the majority of the pilgrims at that time. How, then, has our world so quickly shifted values? How has our world in recent decades decided that behaviors that were sins for thousands of years are no longer sins? How have the teachings of Jesus been so distorted that any Tom, Dick, or Mary can become a pastor and create his or her own church anytime he or she disagrees with what his or her current church is teaching? Has God changed? Have the teachings of Jesus become outdated? Has the format that Jesus and His apostles created over the first few centuries all of a sudden become invalid? Maybe the better question is, Do humans think they are smarter than God? Is our world so different from the world of the Bible that what the Bible teaches us is no longer valid? This is not the case for the same struggles and temptations our ancestors faced. We still face them today: lust, greed, envy, pride, gluttony, anger, and sloth. These sins are the seven deadly sins, and one of these is at the root of every sin. When we speak ill of someone else, it is often rooted in our envy of that person or our own pride, thinking we are better than him or her. When we have sexual desires that cause us to look at pornographic materials, masturbate, commit adultery, or engage in sexual relationships outside of marriage, the sins are rooted in the sin of lust but also can be rooted in envy, gluttony, and sloth.

Often I would hear someone say that the world is changing, thus we have to change with it. This is often an excuse we give when we want to do things we know are wrong. The problem lies in the fact that the more we say this or the more we hear it from others, the more we turn away from God. The more we turn away from God, the harder it is for us to hear our conscious and the Holy Spirit speaking truths to us. Some hikers expressed that the Catholic Church and its rules on human sexuality, abortion, birth control, women being priests, or priestly celibacy were a thing of the past, and if the Church wanted to stay in existence, it would have to change. I do agree that the world is changing, but that does not mean the rules of the natural law have changed or the Church should change. A sin does not stop being a sin because we entered a new decade. Sin today is the same as sin was two thousand years ago, and no matter the number of new civil laws, sin will be the same two thousand years from now.

The use of birth control or other unnatural contraceptives is a sin. The only natural contraceptive not a sin is the natural contraceptive God gave us; it is called our bodies. There are regular times in a woman's body when she is more likely to get pregnant. Being aware of the body that God has given us and using our bodies in the way God intended is what the Church calls Natural Family Planning. The Church has always taught that sex is only between a husband and his wife, and that it should be used to bring the couple in closer union with one another, as well as in closer union as a couple with God. Coming into a closer union with God is when the husband and wife freely say, "Let your will be done," to God, and if it is God's will, the marital act of sex will bring forth new life through a child. It is interesting to note that the teaching on birth control has been accepted in the Christian world by all denominations and only began to change over the last one hundred years. Even if other Christian denominations have chosen to allow this sin into their churches, the Catholic Church has not wavered. Birth control became a Pandora's Box for the Christian world. Viewing birth control as an acceptable practice opened the floodgate for sex outside of marriage, abortion, and homosexual unions. If the God-given purpose of sex is for the union of husband and wife and procreation through God, then when people start using birth control, they begin denying the purpose of sex. When they use birth control, they say, "I want to have sex for pleasure, but I do not want the possibility of a child." Their spouse becomes a sexual object, and they begin using him or her for sexual gratification. Sex that was previously a God-given gift, shared between husband and wife, has now become an act rooted in lust, greed, pride, gluttony, and even laziness.

The world has changed in many ways that have been good and improved the lives of God's people, but we have seen many ways the world has changed for evil. Most of our modern advances in technology are amoral, meaning they, by themselves, are neither good nor evil. Technology will be used for either good or evil based on the intent of the user. So, if I used the Internet to talk with my family while traveling abroad, that is using the Internet for good. If I used the Internet to look up pornographic material for sexual gratification, that is using the Internet for evil. In biblical times, some people were out to make money and twisted truths so that people would follow their paths.

Sounds kind of familiar, huh? Nowadays, in an effort to create money, we are being sold false teachings by being told, "Everyone is doing it," "Organized religion tries to control us," and "If it feels good, how can it be bad?" If we still put up a protest and want to hold fast to our Christian truths, others call us old-fashioned. The media, in an effort to sell products (which are often sin or lead to sin), tells us lies, and after hearing it so much, we slowly allow our guards down. So, when a wolf comes along in sheep's clothing—from a pastor, a teacher, a co-worker, or a family member—we allow those lies to become our false truths, our mottos, and our creeds.

As Christians today, we need to stand on guard to stay true to what God has given us, what Jesus taught us, what the apostles brought to the world, and what the Church has guarded through the centuries. Sin is sin; it does not have an expiration date.

Scripture Meditation: Romans 12:1-2

I urge you therefore, brothers, by the mercies of God, to offer your bodies as a living sacrifice, holy and pleasing to God, your spiritual worship. Do not conform yourselves to this age but be transformed by the renewal of your mind, that you may discern what is the will of God, what is good and pleasing and perfect.

Scripture Meditation: Hebrews 13:7-9

Remember your leaders who spoke the word of God to you. Consider the outcome of their way of life and imitate their faith. Jesus Christ is the same yesterday, today, and forever. Do not be carried away by all kinds of strange teaching.

Scripture Meditation: 2 Timothy 4:1-5

I charge you in the presence of God and of Christ Jesus, who will judge the living and the dead, and by his appearing and his kingly power: proclaim the word; be persistent whether it is convenient or inconvenient; convince, reprimand, encourage through all patience and teaching. For the time will come when people will not tolerate sound doctrine but, following their own desires and insatiable curiosity, will accumulate teachers and will stop listening to the truth and will be diverted to myths. But you, be self-possessed in all circumstances; put up with hardship; perform the work of an evangelist; fulfill your ministry.

Reflection:

Have I softened my view on what I consider to be sin? If so, in what ways have I softened?

Do I think God's commandments or Jesus's teachings are not relevant today? Why or why not?

How can I defend the commandments of God and the teachings of Jesus?

I began this chapter by asking if our world has changed and if the Bible is no longer relevant. Well, if we go to the beginning of the Bible, we read the story of Eden in Genesis 3. Upon further examination we see the sins of Adam and Eve, but we see how it was they came to sin. *Now the snake was the most cunning of all the wild animals that the LORD God had made. He asked the woman, "Did God really say, 'You shall not eat from any of the trees in the garden'?"* At first, Eve did not even see the snake's trap. Had someone said this in a courtroom, a lawyer would have jumped up and objected for leading the witness. Eve, unaware of the trap being laid, stated, *"We may eat of the fruit of the trees in the garden; it is only about the fruit of the tree in the middle of the garden that God said, 'You shall not eat it or even touch it, or else you will die.'"* Then the snake told Eve a lie that made Eve question God's words, *"You certainly will not die! God knows well that when you eat of it your eyes will be opened and you will be like gods, who know good and evil."* We all know how this story ends. The woman gives into sin, and forever the world is changed. The same method used by the snake to lead Eve and Adam to sin is the same method used on us today. The difference is that we know the devil's tricks, and we know the word of God, which prevents us from following in the same footsteps that lead to death.

Lesson 22:

I was a town away from Leon, but from the hilltop of that town, I could see the entire city of Leon. In the middle, I saw the tall towers of the church that stood above the rest of the town. The anticipation on that day of arriving in the city would only compare with my arrival in Santiago. Many times on the Camino, I could see a town but had at least five kilometers to walk before actually getting to it. So, with each step, the anticipation began to build.

The approach to Leon has new streets that include modern buildings. In the old town, the narrow cobblestone roads twist and turn, because the town built the newer roads around the older buildings. I was tired and had been taking medicine to get over a cold, but as I entered the old streets of Leon, I forgot all of that. The excitement continued to build, because I saw many people I had grown close with on the Camino or had shared meaningful conversations with. In addition, the town was hosting its annual festival in honor of Saint Froilan, the patron saint for the town, and the streets were full of vendors and spectators. The streets were winding, and I never knew at what point I would arrive at the Cathedral.

Upon arriving at the Cathedral, I understood a lesson that God was teaching me. He had used the Camino towns as visual aids. The walk into towns on the Camino parallels our walks in this life. In the town before Leon, had I walked a straight line through the town to get to the Cathedral, I would have walked half of the distance, but I would have had to find a way to walk through buildings. On the other hand, by walking around the buildings, I took many winding streets and spent twice as long getting to the church. That extra time walking built up the anticipation I was feeling. The same way that celebrating the season of Advent builds up our anticipation for the coming of Christ or a mother spends nine months in anticipation for the birth of her child. Upon arrival at the Cathedral, I was excited and ready to enter. In the same way, my faith journey, as well as the faith journeys of most people I know, has not been a straight path to God. I had to take a few winding roads to get to God, and as I got closer, I noticed the road became narrower like the small cobblestone streets leading to the Cathedral.

Scripture Meditation: Matthew 7:13-14

"Enter through the narrow gate; for the gate is wide and the road broad that leads to destruction, and those who enter through it are many. How narrow the gate and constricted the road that leads to life. And those who find it are few."

Reflection:

When in life have I taken a direct path to God?

When have I taken a winding road to God? How did taking a winding road strengthen my desire for God?

When in my faith journey have I been on a narrow road, drawing closer to God?

God made us in His image, and He placed in our hearts the desire to know Him. Life can be confusing like the winding streets, but when we have God in the center, life just seems to make sense. We cannot know the hour of our deaths, so none of us can intentionally take a winding road to place God in the center of life. But many people find they take a winding road once or twice. I am thankful for the winding roads I have taken, because they have brought me to God and removed the sin of pride, which I am prone to. Of course looking back, I wish I had not needed to take a winding road. I encourage the youth I work with to stay on the straight and narrow road to God, but I also recognize that my love for God, personally, would not be where it is today had I not taken that winding road.

Lesson 23:

I walked through the winding streets guided by streetlights as I departed Leon in the early morning hours. The streets were a complete contrast to the festival the day before. There was silence in the streets, and I only saw a pair of nuns walking around the town. About six kilometers after leaving the monastery, I came to a bar and went in to get a bite to eat. Behind the counter I saw an item that I had not had since starting my pilgrimage, and I had an instant hunger for it. It was a donut. I placed my backpack in a chair, ordered the donut, and went to use the restroom. I returned to my table where the donut was on a plate, and I did the strangest thing. I took some napkins, wrapped the donut up, placed my backpack on, and began walking. For breakfast I would usually eat part of a baguette from the previous day, a piece of fruit, or a cereal bar, but every now and then upon passing a bakery or on a rainy day, I would stop at a bar or café for a pastry or hot chocolate. I always ate the item there or ate the item as I literally walked out the door. But for some reason, I wrapped this item up, even though I was hungry and it looked good.

Within two minutes of the bar was a very small chapel I had not seen before, and the front door was open. I crossed the street and read the flyer on the door, which told me a Mass would be starting in ten minutes. I entered the small chapel (room for about thirty), took off my backpack, and smiled, because God had been leading me through the Holy Spirit when I had a feeling to wrap up that donut. For by unintentionally fasting prior to the Mass, I was able to participate and be nourished by Jesus in the Eucharist. Though a donut was exciting (yes, on the

Camino I really learned to appreciate very simple things) it did not compare to the excitement my heart had when I received Jesus in the Eucharist.

I did not always believe nor understand the teaching of the Eucharist. The truth that the body, blood, soul, and divinity of Jesus Christ are really present in the Eucharist was a concept I had never learned or studied. For upon studying, but more importantly through prayer, this truth and teaching of Jesus, the apostles, and the Church became my reality. This reality is the greatest gift I have ever been given, as well as the source I go to for strength. To many people, the thought of the Eucharist being Christ's body and blood turns them away from the church. The same was true in Jesus's day. In the Bible, we see His teaching in Chapter 6 of John, and His disciples responded, "*This is a hard saying. Who can accept it?*" Jesus goes on to tell them that many do not believe and cannot accept this teaching. Verse 66 says, "*As a result of this, many [of] his disciples returned to their former way of life and no longer accompanied him.*" Jesus then asked His twelve apostles if they also wanted to leave. To that Simon Peter answered, "*Master, to whom shall we go? You have the words of eternal life. We have come to believe and are convinced that you are the Holy One of God.*"

Scripture Meditation John 6:48-58

I am the bread of life. Your ancestors ate the manna in the desert, but they died; this is the bread that comes down from heaven so that one may eat it and not die. I am the living bread that came down from heaven; whoever eats this bread will live forever; and the bread that I will give is my flesh for the life of the world." The Jews quarreled among themselves, saying, "How can this man give us [his] flesh to eat?" Jesus said to them, "Amen, amen, I say to you, unless you eat the flesh of the Son of Man and drink his blood, you do not have life within you. Whoever eats my flesh and drinks my blood has eternal life, and I will raise him on the last day. For my flesh is true food, and my blood is true drink. Whoever eats my flesh and drinks my blood remains in me and I in him. Just as the living Father sent me and I have life because of the Father, so also the one who feeds on me will have life because of me. This is the bread that came down from heaven. Unlike your ancestors who ate and still died, whoever eats this bread will live forever.

Reflection:

What teachings of the Lord do I struggle with?

Do I have a donut story—a time when the Holy Spirit led me? How can I have more of these stories?

I could not have told you why I walked into a café to order food to eat and then wrapped it up to leave, but God knew the reason beforehand. After Mass that morning, God so filled me that I walked for about two hours before I ever ate that donut, and I never felt hungry. We must trust in God and allow His Holy Spirit to love us, provide good gifts for us, and nourish us. The miracle of the donut is a small example of the Holy Spirit working and the Eucharist being a source of nourishment.

Lesson 24:

One day as I walked alone, I thought about the many stories I had heard from pilgrims about why they walked the Camino, and I had a profound thought. Ignore all the things that make us different (age, gender, nationality, religion, and so on). In reality, there are only two types of people: those who love God first and those who love themselves first.

When we love God first, we are following His call to His commandments. Jesus tells His followers in Chapter 22 of Matthew, "*You shall love the Lord, your God, with all your heart, with all your soul, and with all your mind. This is the greatest and the first commandment.*" When Jesus spoke to people who were falling short in their spiritual lives, He got two responses from them: either they went away sad like the rich man who loved himself more than God, or they gained happiness by converting their lives to loving God first.

Often we see people who strive to live Christian lives, but their love of self prevents them from loving God first. Just like many of you, this is a battle that I wage everyday— loving God first before I love myself. In our culture today, it is all about our self-image, the clothes we wear, the cars we drive, the homes we live in, being the best in our fields, and the gadgets we have, and the list of self-improvement continues. Ever notice how many books in a bookstore are on self-improvement? Do you think a bookstore—a business set up for profit—would dedicate that much shelf space if people were not buying those books? Just another piece of our cultural war, where society tells me how to focus on myself instead of God. Now, I am not speaking ill of self-improvement books, as I am sure many people have received great benefit from them, but I will bet my money that the Bible has done greater things for more people than any self-improvement book ever written.

God is love, and through the Trinity—the Father, the Son, and the Holy Spirit—we are given insight into what perfect love looks like. We have also seen what the gift of true love looks like in a very graphic way through the gospel stories of Jesus's passion. True love is a giving love; it is not a taking love. Jesus did not ask what we would do for Him if He suffered humiliation and gave up His life for our sins.

I find it ironic that the people I know who love God above themselves seem to often have a higher love of themselves than the people who choose first to love themselves above God. How can that be? Well, I think that when we love the creator, how can we not love His creation? If you have ever had a little sibling, a child, a niece, or a nephew, or been around a young child when he or she starts drawing, you will understand this. The artwork is often unrecognizable, and the child usually has to tell you what he or she has drawn, but because you love the creator of that artwork, you love the art. Many parents proudly display that art around their home or office because they love the artist. On the other hand, many people who seek to love themselves first instead of God are often unhappy. They are lacking the joy and peace that comes from true love. By deciding to not love God first, since God is the very person that is love, they never know in their own lives the true love that comes with loving Him. This is where lust can be confused for love. They lust after pleasing themselves through money, things, and people, and although they might call it love, they will never know the true meaning of love outside of God.

Scripture Meditation: Mark 12:30-31

'You shall love the Lord your God with all your heart, with all your soul, with all your mind, and with all your strength.' The second is this: 'You shall love your neighbor as yourself.' There is no other commandment greater than these.

Reflection:

Whom do I love first in my life?

What are some ways that I have placed love of myself above my love of God?

What will help me the most in my daily struggle to love God above myself?

When we love God, we love ourselves, because God created us. We also love our neighbors, because God also created them. When we love our neighbors, we are no longer envious of the gifts they possess but, instead, give thanks to God that they have certain gifts we do not. For, if I had every gift in the world, I would not need anyone else. I could do it all by myself, but instead, God has intentionally connected us to Himself and our communities.

Lesson 25:

The Camino is a lot of things for many people, but one thing it is not is a fashion trip. Pilgrims are always wearing the same clothes. Most pilgrims have two outfits, and a few will bring three. So, each day they hike in one outfit, and then after a shower, they change into the other outfit to wear to bed (while the other outfit dries on a clothesline) and then hike in the following day. The weight of a backpack is important for pilgrims, so when packing as well as on the trail, they scrutinize the items to make sure each one is necessary. So, hair products, make-up, dress clothes, or anything they would normally use to make themselves attractive get left at home. I did not pack lotion because I did not think it was a necessity. But after my feet cracked, I learned it was and picked up the smallest bottle I could find at a store.

I found it interesting that on the Camino, we left behind many products that were not necessary and felt could weigh us down physically. Yet, in life, we often carry around many things that help us put up fake images of who we are, which can weigh us down emotionally. The Camino gave pilgrims chances to meet people who were raw and real, and they met them exactly where they were at that stage in their lives. We shared our dreams and our tragedies and about why we hiked. We only saw the person who was standing before us. We saw who they really were—their interiors. Outside of the Camino, when we meet people, we meet the people they want to project— through the way they dress, the cars they drive, the phones they have, the hairstyles, and the information they share. Usually all of that is exterior, and rarely do we meet people who let us into their interiors. On the Camino, some women did wear makeup, but the majority of women did not. I thought about how we use makeup to enhance our facial features or to cover up our facial features, but either way, we do not project the image as it is, but as we want the world to see it.

A gift of the Camino was meeting people for who they were and not judging them based on their crazy windblown hair (this was me), the natural odor of their bodies, or if they snored at night. We met them where they were and loved them no matter how different they were from us. I heard, once upon a time in a leadership seminar, that the average person spends three months in a relationship trying to impress the other person. That means that we put our best foot forward, trying to be the person that the other person wants us to be. Then we slowly share our real selves with that person. Is it just me, or does this bother you? Does it seem like we spend a lot of our life pretending? Think of the people you truly love. Most likely, you have shown them who you really are, and in turn, they have shared their interior selves with you. If this has yet to occur, then it is not a loving relationship. How can a loving relationship be built around a fake image that someone has created?

I invite you to examine your own life and ask yourself who your real relationships are. They are the relationships in which you have an interior connection with. Who are your superficial exterior relationships? Consider weeding out the superficial relationships in your life. They drain you of your time and energy, because you have to put forward the idea of pretending to be someone else. When seedlings begin coming through the soil, a gardener removes some so the other ones will have more space to grow healthy. That is also true of our relationships; we have to weed out the superficial and bad relationships to allow the real and good relationships to grow.

Scripture Meditation: 1 Corinthians 15:33

Do not be led astray: "Bad company corrupts good morals."

Reflection:

Do I have a superficial relationship that I need to let go?

Are there people I should increase my relationship with because they draw me closer to God?

Are there things about me I can change to stop putting so much time into building a superficial image?

Many people are afraid to remove superficial relationships from their lives because those relationships offer them popularity and comfort, or they are afraid of being alone. At the end of the day, I would rather spend my time trying to please God in His company than spend my time trying to impress a superficial relationship. A superficial relationship will choke not only good relationships in my life, but it will also choke my spiritual life, because the superficial relationship has me focus on worldly things.

Lesson 26:

The flat section was over, and the inclines and declines had started again. I found it symbolic as I approached a cross statue with the mountain inclines in the background. By this point, my groin was pulled, and I knew that, with the inclines and declines to come, the pain was about to get even more intense, yet I found comfort upon seeing the cross. I knew that every day I was called to arise and carry my cross, and that Jesus himself carried His cross for my salvation and for the salvation of the world. The crosses we have will never be too great for us if we carry them for the love of Christ, as Christ carried His cross for His love of us. So, by carrying my cross for the love of God, He gave me the strength and grace I needed, no matter how high the mountain gets.

Scripture Meditation: Luke 9:23

Then he said to all, "If anyone wishes to come after me, he must deny himself and take up his cross daily and follow me."

Reflection:

When have I struggled to accept the cross that God has given me?

Would others say I lovingly take up my cross, or do I complain about it?

Crosses come in many shapes and sizes; sometimes our cross is a job, a person, an illness, an injury, or a situation. We never know what physical shape our crosses will take or how large or small they might appear. Every person has a cross, and each person deals differently with the cross they are given. Over our lifetimes, we will have many different crosses. The last time I saw my grandmother, she was in pain on her deathbed, struggling to breathe. She embraced her cross and gave praise to God. She was a prime example of using her cross to encourage and strengthen others with their own crosses in their faith journeys.

Lesson 27:

In high school I played golf for a couple of years, and I learned how to gauge the distance to the green so I would know which club to use. In my career, working in residence life, I learn to gauge the distance of hallways to replace flooring. Neither of these special skills helped me to gauge how far away a town was while I was walking. On the Camino, I was often deceived, thinking that the town ahead of me was a lot closer than it was. This was one of the harder things on the Camino. My eyes would see a town, and then my entire body would respond. I suddenly had the urge to go to the restroom, I was thinking what I might get to eat, and my feet were ready for a break. During the flat parts, especially on clear days, I could see for a great distance. I would see a town, but it might take another two or three hours before I would actually arrive to the center of the town. What had seemed so close ended up taking me two hours to get to, where I could rest and get food before hiking on to the next town.

As I walked and thought about how far away the town was, I thought of my former students. During my career, I have had many conversations with high school and college students who believed in God, knew the basics of His teachings, and called themselves Christians but were unwilling to submit to His teachings. They often knew that some of their actions were sinful, but they excused them by believing they were "only young once." Most felt confident in the fact that they would have fun then, living the lives they were living but would live Christian lives as they got older, married, and began having children. You see, for many of those teens, they thought they could ignore God and His rules during the early part of their lives because they would have time later on to make amends for their ways. When the reality is, not one of us has a guarantee for today, let alone tomorrow.

A few times on the Camino, when I was walking up and down in a mountain area, a town would appear out of nowhere; the mountains had hidden the town from sight. I would walk to the top of a mountain and immediately see a town right there on the other side. When I was thirteen years old, my childhood, best friend died in a car accident. I remember being at the funeral and hearing the Priest talk about her, and I sat in that church wondering why her and not me. She was a better person than I was. At that age I could not answer, why her and not me? And two decades later, I still cannot answer that question. What I do know is that her earthly life was cut short.

In the same way, each one of us could die this very day. So, the idea that in youth we can make mistakes now and correct them as adults is misleading. I wish I could tell you I have never sinned, but I cannot. I can tell you that I am thankful that God allowed me to keep living, so that I could turn toward Him and focus my life on Him. Allowing us to live is God's gift to us. Choosing to follow God's way is our gift to God. Do not squander your life, living your life as if you have time to enter the Kingdom of Heaven. The reality is that the Kingdom of God is already here.

Scripture Meditation: James 4:13-15

Come now, you who say, "Today or tomorrow we shall go into such and such a town, spend a year there doing business, and make a profit" you have no idea what your life will be like tomorrow. You are a puff of smoke that appears briefly and then disappears. Instead you should say, "If the Lord wills it, we shall live to do this or that."

Reflection:

What would God say about the decisions I make each day?

Do I ever think about my death and each day as a gift?

How can I live everyday like it is a gift from God?

My friend, strive to live your life as if each day was your last and what you do today will determine where you will spend eternity. Imagine what the world would look like if each Christian lived his or her life like this.

Lesson 28:

I was walking into a town as I heard church bells at one of the churches. Because all the churches did not have bells ringing, I knew that meant it was time for Mass. I went to Mass, and the gospel reading was from Luke. The gospel was the perfect message for Mass, as well as for me to reflect on the rest of the day as I walked.

The gospel story was about a man asking Jesus what he needed to do to have eternal life. Jesus asked him what the law said to do, and the man told Jesus, "*You shall love the Lord, your God, with all your heart, with all your being, with all your strength, and with all your mind, and your neighbor as yourself.*" Jesus told the man that what he had said was right and told him to go live his life following those laws.

Now, this is the part of the story I love, because I could see myself asking Jesus the same follow up question the man did, "*And who is my neighbor?*" Of course, Jesus did not say everyone to the young man. Instead, he told a story— the story of the Good Samaritan. At the end of the story, Jesus asked the question, who was the neighbor? The man understood completely that everyone is our neighbor, and anyone we see in need of help is whom we are called to help.

The Camino offered me the opportunity to meet people from all over the world; every continent was represented except for Antarctica. Pilgrims represented the world community. I did not meet anyone on the Camino whom I knew before my trip, but on the trail, each person became my neighbor. Anywhere I looked on the Camino, I saw the Good Samaritan story coming to life. There was the Italian doctor who told me what was wrong with my foot, the Spaniard who shared her cream to help the inflammation, and the New Zealand couple who gave me some pain medicine until I could get to a pharmacy. In the same way, I was able to share my medicine with a Canadian and give my ankle brace to another American who was in greater need. Of course, taking care of one another was not restricted to medicine. We helped through offering encouraging words, letting someone in greater need have a bottom bunk, sharing the food we had with one another, and slowing down to walk with other pilgrims who were physically struggling. These are just a few of the ways that we were able to care for one another as good neighbors.

Imagine what the world would look like if we lived our days looking for opportunities to be Good Samaritans to those we come in contact with. Without even having conversations, if we saw someone limping, we would offer what we had. The world of the Camino was made up of people striving to reach the same destination and wanting to make sure the other pilgrims could reach it as well. Our earthly goal is to reach heaven and to help other people reach heaven as well, and the Camino was the perfect road map showing us how to do that.

Scripture Meditation: Luke 10:25 - 37

There was a scholar of the law who stood up to test him and said, "Teacher, what must I do to inherit eternal life?" Jesus said to him, "What is written in the law? How do you read it?" He said in reply, "You shall love the Lord, your God, with all your heart, with all your being, with all your strength, and with all your mind, and your neighbor as yourself." He replied to him, "You have answered correctly; do this and you will live." But because he wished to justify himself, he said to Jesus, "And who is my neighbor?" Jesus replied, "A man fell victim to robbers as he went down from Jerusalem to Jericho. They stripped and beat him and went off leaving him half-dead. A priest happened to be going down that road, but when he saw him, he passed by on the opposite side. Likewise a Levite came to the place, and when he saw him, he passed by on the opposite side. But a Samaritan traveler who came upon him was moved with compassion at the sight. He approached the victim, poured oil and wine over his wounds and bandaged them. Then he lifted him up on his own animal, took him to an inn and cared for him. The next day he took out two silver coins and gave them to the innkeeper with the instruction, 'Take care of him. If you spend more than what I have given you, I shall repay you on my way back.' Which of these three, in your opinion, was neighbor to the robbers' victim?" He answered, "The one who treated him with mercy." Jesus said to him, "Go and do likewise."

Reflection:

Who in my life is a Good Samaritan? What is it about him or her that makes me describe that person as a Good Samaritan?

What is one thing I can do today for someone I do not know?

I met a man from California that I ended up walking about the same distance with each day, so we often saw one another at evening Mass. He often passed me and knew that my injuries were causing me to walk slowly, but he was also feeling the pain and doing the "pilgrim shuffle" at nighttime. One night as I was leaving Mass, he told me we would make Santiago, and I said, "If it is God's will, I will get there."

Then he said, "If needed, I will drag you there!" What would it look like if we all showed each other that level of commitment? Especially to someone we had just met. Being a good neighbor is all about looking for opportunities to serve others at all times, even when we might need a good neighbor ourselves. I challenge you to make a personal goal to do one Good Samaritan act every day of your life. It can be as simple as opening a door for someone. Even small acts can have a lasting impact.

Lesson 29:

We were walking in the mountains, and the second small town we passed through did not have a café, bar, or grocery store to get food. A Spanish-speaking pilgrim was walking the opposite way, asking if anyone had seen a café and motioning to his mouth. As I passed him, I handed him a cereal bar from my pack so he could have something to eat, since there was nothing open. I continued walking, and a guy from Texas, who had seen my Good Samaritan act, struck up a conversation with me. This led to a two-hour faith conversation. Texas was walking the Camino with his seventy-five-year-old father. He wanted me to meet his father that evening, since we were going to be staying in the same town.

I arrived at the town early and had to wait until the check-in time at the albergue, so I went to the other albergue in town that had a bar to get a hot tea, since it was another cold and rainy day. Inside the bar were Texas and his father. They were staying at this albergue, so the three of us sat there sharing our faith and life stories. After a couple hours, some friends they had made on the trail joined us at our table. The woman was Irish, and the man was Dutch. After introductions, Ireland was moving around her papers when the father saw something that caught his eye. It was a Jesus Prayer Card, and the father asked Ireland if he could see it. Ireland handed the father the prayer card and then began sharing that she had found it on the trail and was not sure what to do with it. Texas's head went down into his hands, and I could tell what was happening, but Ireland kept talking. Ireland told us she thought the prayer card was lovely, but that someone had lost it, so she was thinking about placing it at the foot of the cross for the person to hopefully find. At that point, the Dutchman interrupted, saying that she had talked about it all day. Texas's head rose up, and the father was shaking the card in his hand, so Ireland and the Dutchman understood that Texas was the person who had lost the card.

This one act of providence then triggered the Dutchman to share that he, too, had lost something on the Camino. A friend had given him a rosary, and on the very first day of his pilgrimage, he had lost it. Immediately, as the Dutchman was telling us this, I felt the Holy Spirit guide me. I placed my hand in my pocket and felt my rosary. After he finished talking, I pulled the rosary from my pocket and handed it to the Dutchman. I told him that my faith community back home had made it, and I knew that it was meant for him. After a few minutes, the Dutchman and Ireland decided to take a walk to the mountain cross to see the cross at sunset, so they left. I also left to check into my albergue, as it was now past the time that they were accepting pilgrims. I headed up to the church albergue.

After showering, cleaning my clothes, and setting up my bed for the evening, I walked around the very small town and ended up at the albergue bar, where Texas and his father were sitting at the table talking. We were probably talking for another two hours when I felt the Dutchman's arms come around my body and give me a hug and then a kiss on my cheek. The Dutchman said that he had asked God for a sign that day because he did not feel like life was worth living, and that losing his rosary at the start of the pilgrimage felt like a bad sign. Then a complete stranger handed him a rosary, and he knew it was a sign from God that God was still there, and he was to live.

My action of giving a stranger my rosary was a small action, yet it had a profound impact on the man's life. We never know how the things we do or say will impact other people, but when we feel led by the Holy Spirit, we only need to trust that God has His reason. I am sure that throughout my entire life, God has been trying to talk to me and guide me through His Holy Spirit, but so often, I was not listening. The Holy Spirit is with each of us, we just need to allow ourselves to be open to hear what He is trying to tell us. I wish God used billboards, but that is usually not His style. I have found that God's style for me is speaking so softly that it is a whisper I feel down in my soul. But if I allow noise in my life and get caught up in distractions, I miss what His whisper is telling me to do.

Allowing the Holy Spirit to guide our lives will allow us to do things that are humanly impossible, but of course, for God, all things are possible. God chose that rosary and me to be an instrument for the Dutchman. All I had to do was listen and then allow God to use me.

Scripture Meditation: John 14:16-18

And I will ask the Father, and he will give you another Advocate to be with you always, the Spirit of truth, which the world cannot accept, because it neither sees nor knows it. But you know it, because it remains with you, and will be in you. I will not leave you orphans; I will come to you.

Reflection:

When in my life have I felt the Holy Spirit moving me?
How did I respond?

How do I keep noise and distractions away so that I can
hear when God is speaking to me?

One of my fears about returning to America and getting
involved again was that I might allow distractions and
noise to overtake my life. Going on a pilgrimage or retreat
is great, but if I return and fall back into the same old
pattern, then I defeat the purpose of the experience. This
is why I have to stay on guard for my spiritual life. I have
to protect my prayer time with God and not allow the
noise of everyday life to confuse me or the message God
desires me to hear. It is hard. On my pilgrimage, both the
parts on and off the Camino, I found it easy to know
exactly where God wanted me, what He wanted me to do,
and what He wanted me to say. Once I returned to the
states, I found I had to spend a lot more time in prayer to
understand His will. A lot of this had to do with my failure
to stay in a continuous state of prayer and allowing
distractions like a movie or TV show to pull me away.

Lesson 30:

On the Camino near the end, a cross on a mountaintop has a pile of rocks under it. Upon arrival at the cross, pilgrims leave rocks from home. I woke up early to leave the albergue I was staying at so I could get to the cross before sunrise. I walked in complete blackness up the mountain trail and arrived at the cross while it was still dark. I was at the cross for a good hour before any other pilgrims came. On a bench, I sat thinking about the rock in my hand and about what it meant to me.

The rock I had brought from home had a story of its own. I had randomly received the rock on a retreat the year before, and the rock had the word "submit" on it. The word submit corresponded to the Bible verse I was given at that retreat. James 4:7 says, "*Submit yourselves to God. Resist the devil, and he will flee from you.*" For the entire three months prior to that retreat, I had been under the most intense spiritual warfare of my life. That rock became a physical item that represented a spiritual battle I had just undergone with the devil.

I had carried that rock with me on my pilgrimage, and now I prayed alone in the dark at the foot of the cross. My prayers were of thanksgiving for God bringing me through that trial in my life, for the gift He had given me of the pilgrimage, and for the freedom He had given me from my burdens. As I placed that rock at the foot of the cross, I literally thought I was taking my burdens and giving them over to Jesus. Our burdens and sins, like my twenty-seven-pound backpack, can weigh us down, and God does not desire that for us. In addition, as I sat at the foot of the cross, I also realized I was submitting 100 percent to God's will and doing whatever He desired me to do.

Scripture Meditation: James 4:7

Submit yourselves to God. Resist the devil, and he will flee from you.

Reflection:

What do the words submit yourself to God mean to me?

Am I willing to submit my entire life over to God?

The word submit in our secular culture has a negative connotation. I will admit there have been very few bosses in my career I have wanted to submit to. However, when I think in the context of submitting to God, it seems like a no-brainer. Why would I ever want to not submit to God? By submitting to God, I enter into a relationship with Him where I tell Him I trust Him, I need Him, I will do what He wants me to do, and I think He knows best. The most precious gift I have is myself, and I have freely given this to God. Submitting to God feels right, but I spent a lot of time afraid of submitting because of what He might ask of me. So, I understand your fear, but if you sit at the foot of a cross or crucifix, I think you will understand His love for you.

Lesson 31:

The mountain was like a fall morning: a bit cool and covered in fog. The day before the sun was out, and I could see a great distance on the mountain, but today we could only see a little bit ahead. The fog reminded me of the mystery of God. So often, we want to know our futures, but the fog is a great reminder that we cannot know that far ahead. Instead of trying to see our futures, we should focus on the current day and what we can see. There is nothing wrong with planning for our futures; we just need to make sure the plans we are making are God's plans for us.

While we live on this earth, I do not think we will ever see the big picture of our lives—how all the parts come together. Just like the mountain, parts of our lives and the impact our lives have had on others will remain in fog. Only when we are with the Creator will we understand and be able to see clearly. Do not get sad because you cannot see the big picture, but instead, rejoice in the mystery.

Scripture Meditation: Jeremiah 29:11-14

For I know well the plans I have in mind for you, says the LORD, plans for your welfare, not for woe! plans to give you a future full of hope. When you call me, when you go to pray to me, I will listen to you. When you look for me, you will find me. Yes, when you seek me with all your heart, you will find me with you...

Reflection:

How does not knowing my future worry me?

How can I trust in the plans the Lord has made for my life?

I was always a planner, and once I began trying to live my life for God, I became a worrier. I thought I should be living the vocation God desired for me, but I did not know which vocation God desired for me. Part of my pilgrimage was to get away and discover what God was calling me to, be it religious life, married life, or committed single life. The lesson of the fog is that God will reveal in His time and not my timeline. This lesson became a beautiful gift, because it allowed me to not stress about my vocation and doing God's will. Instead, I accept the fog each day and follow what I can clearly see that God wants me to do. As for the stuff that hides behind the fog, I leave that to my prayer time with God.

Lesson 32:

Upon arrival at an albergue, I would always ask if there would be a Mass and at what time it would begin. On this night, the volunteers running the albergue let me know that the Mass would be at the convent church and told me what time to meet to go with the other pilgrims staying at the albergue.

Out of the twenty pilgrims staying there, the majority of us went to the Mass. For many it was their first Mass of the Camino. For one Swede it would be his first Mass experience ever. As we entered the convent, the nuns were praying the rosary on the right side of the chapel, and our group began sitting on the left side of the chapel. Since my groin was pulled at this point, I was walking slowly, so I entered near the back of our group. The albergue volunteer that had come with us was acting as an usher and showing the pilgrims to their seats. Since no pilgrims had sat in the first pew, he pointed to the Swede and me to take that pew, which we did.

As Mass began, I realized the Swede was unsure as to what was happening and was always standing or sitting a step behind everyone else. So when it came time for the readings, I shared with him the missal readings. After the Liturgy of the Word, it was time for the Liturgy of the Eucharist, and this is where I saw the Swede making great effort as he paid attention to what was happening at the altar. Following the Lord's Prayer, I turned to the Swede, took his hand, and said, "Peace be with you." I naturally speak really fast, and seeing the confused look on his face, I once again said, "Peace be with you." This time I spoke very slowly and deliberately, making solid eye contact as I held his hand. This mountain man from Switzerland that stood at least a foot taller than me radiated the most beautiful smile as I gave him the sign of peace. Then I turned around to wish the albergue volunteer and the Frenchwoman who sat behind us the sign of peace, and the Swede followed suit. After that, this man, who at the beginning of Mass had a worrisome look on his face, now radiated light from his interior that showed through to his exterior.

I had never realized what a gift it was to look at someone in the eye and to wish him peace. Yet, I was not just wishing this man peace but also really wishing for the peace of our Lord to come upon him. When Christ returned following His resurrection, the very first words He shared, when all His disciples were together, were, "Peace be with you," from John 20. Every part of the Mass is very intentional, and every part of the Mass dates back to Christ and the early Church. The man from Switzerland, attending his very first Mass, taught me the essence of the meaning of the sign of peace. We are to offer and receive Christ's peace with joy and to allow His peace to rest upon us.

Spiritual Meditation: John 14:27

"Peace I leave with you; my peace I give to you. Not as the world gives do I give it to you. Do not let your hearts be troubled or afraid."

Reflection:

When have I felt God's peace?

In my spiritual life, when have I allowed a habit to become routine and lose its meaning?

Never allow yourself to let God's gift of giving and receiving His peace to become a habit, where you simply start going through the motions of Mass. We are all like the Swede, and we all have our troubles. If we do not pay attention, we can miss the joy that Christ is offering us in His gift of peace.

Lesson 33:

Many of the albergues along the Camino were established by the Parish church, religious lay organizations, and the monasteries of the religious orders that open up their homes to pilgrims. As a rule, I tried to stay at an albergue associated with the Catholic Church if there was one available in the town. The private albergues usually had the best amenities with the smallest number of pilgrims in a room but had the highest prices. The municipal albergues were about the same price as the Catholic albergues, but the municipals usually offered a few extra amenities. The Catholic albergues were very basic. They were open to pilgrims of all faiths, usually a bit drafty from being in ancient buildings, and usually offered a Mass or prayer service.

At most services, before they began or at the conclusion, the priests would ask what languages people spoke and give them guidebooks to use during the service or prayer cards in their native languages. Then different pilgrims would take part in the prayer service in their native languages. This was always special because it would remind me that the words Catholic Church mean universal church, and we have members all over the world.

At the Saint Nicholas albergue during the pilgrim prayer service, we heard the gospel reading that tells us Jesus is the vine, we are the branches, and God is the vine grower. Then as God would have it, on the very next day, I found myself hiking in the mountains surrounded by vineyards, so I meditated on the gospel I had heard the day before. That was yet another blessing on the Camino where I got to watch God work, because it had been probably ten days since I had seen a vineyard. It truly was remarkable that after hearing Jesus's teaching on the vineyards, I found myself in the middle of vineyards that went on for as far as my eyes could see, in all directions. It literally felt like on my pilgrimage, God was constantly giving me visual aids so that I could remember His teachings. God is good!

As I walked along the path surrounded by the vineyards, I meditated on the gospel reading and looked at the abundance of grapes that were in season—almost ripe for picking. I thought that we, too, are in abundance, and the closer we remain to Christ, the more we grow and bear fruit. In addition to the abundance of healthy grape bunches on the vines, I also noticed bunches of grapes on the ground that had either fallen by themselves or had been picked by a passerby to eat but then tossed on the ground to decay, as they were not ripe yet. How true is this about our own spiritual lives? When we stay connected to Jesus, "the vine," He nourishes us, and we receive the gifts we need to survive. The grapes sometimes fall off on their own, and this is when we choose to leave God, thinking we can do better on our own. I have never known someone who has walked away from God and not seen the decay in his or her life shortly thereafter. In the same way, sometimes we are trying to stay connected to God, but then someone else comes along and we allow someone to pull us away. And if we do not repent and strive to go back to God, we will decay too. Then there are the times when God tries to pull us back to Him, but we ignore Him, so to help us, He cuts himself from us. If God cuts us from the vine but we repent and strive to reunite with Him, He welcomes us back as a prodigal son, and we have a reconversion. This is when we see the grape on the ground separated from the vine and in decay. Through our repentance, we are converted and brought back to God. We die to our old sinful ways and are reborn. This, of course, is a process where a grape decays and reenters the soil to be reunited with the vine. This process is more painful than simply staying connected to the vine in the first place, but it is a process of mercy and forgiveness that our Father gives us to reunite us to His kingdom.

Scripture Meditation: John 15:1-9

"I am the true vine, and my Father is the vine grower. He takes away every branch in me that does not bear fruit, and everyone that does he prunes so that it bears more fruit. You are already pruned because of the word that I spoke to you. Remain in me, as I remain in you. Just as a branch cannot bear fruit on its own unless it remains on the vine, so neither can you unless you remain in me. I am the vine, you are the branches. Whoever remains in me and I in him will bear much fruit, because without me you can do nothing. Anyone who does not remain in me will be thrown out like a branch and wither; people will gather them and throw them into a fire and they will be burned. If you remain in me and my words remain in you, ask for whatever you want and it will be done for you. By this is my Father glorified, that you bear much fruit and become my disciples. As the Father loves me, so I also love you. Remain in my love."

Reflection:

What fruit am I currently bearing in my life because I am connected to Jesus?

If God has ever cut me from the vine, how did that feel, and what brought me back to the vine?

No one can bear fruit without the vine grower (God) and staying connected through His vine (Jesus). Sometimes we get so busy serving others and trying to serve God's will that we drift away from nourishing ourselves. If we are failing to receive fully what Jesus has to offer us, then we cannot bear the multitude of fruit that God desires for us. In your own faith journey, stay nourished and connected to God, the source of life.

Lesson 34:

On the morning of October 13, I was praying my rosary and walking up the mountain when the sun began to rise. I was at the top of the mountain and had a clear view of the rising sun, because I was on the tallest peak in the area. This date in history was the date that the miracle of the dancing sun occurred in Fatima, which many parts of Europe could see. I thought about not only the universal connection of believers of today, but also how we are connected to all of God's people, including those who are now in heaven. It also gave me a chance to reflect on Mary's role in Christianity. Prior to my pilgrimage, theologically I could explain Mary's role, but I am not sure if my brain and heart were connected. My pilgrimage led me to many sites where Marian apparitions occurred, and on this morning, I reflected on her role.

God chose Mary to be the instrument, a tabernacle to bring salvation to the world, offered through Jesus Christ. God could have chosen to have Jesus descend to earth as a thirty-year-old man, but God did not choose that path. Instead, God chose to use Mary, and through the Holy Spirit, she carried inside of her a baby. She raised Jesus, and He spent His first thirty years with her before beginning His ministry. The very first miracle documented in the Bible was a miracle that Mary requested on behalf of a bride and groom. Reading the Wedding of Cana in Chapter 2 of John, the account appears to have Jesus speaking down to His mother when He says, "*Woman, how does your concern affect me? My hour has not yet come.*" But the Bible was not written using our modern language style, and we see that, without any hesitation, Mary knew her son was going to fix the problem, so she told the servants to do exactly as He instructed. To also understand that Jesus meant no disrespect when He called Mary "woman," we can look at the tender exchange of an only son on His deathbed, making sure His mother would be provided for after His death. The author of John, in Chapter 19, shared the last exchange between Jesus, His mother, and His beloved disciple before He died on the cross. "*When Jesus saw his mother and the disciple there whom he loved, he said to his mother, 'Woman, behold, your son.' Then he said to the disciple, 'Behold, your mother.' And from that hour the disciple took her into his home.*" So, clearly, the term woman was a term of affection, and Jesus cared greatly for His mother and wanted to ensure she was cared for after He was no longer on earth.

In these two Bible verses, we see that Mary intercedes on our behalf to her son, and holds a special place in her son's heart. In the Marian apparitions approved by the Catholic Church, Mary is always drawing people to her son and encouraging them to turn to God. As a result, we have seen thousands of people turn away from sin and turn to God. In addition, the sites of Marian apparitions have become sites of pilgrimages, and the messages often transform communities, countries, and those who visit the sites.

That evening I arrived at my albergue and started settling into my bunk when the woman in the bunk next to me told me we had met before. I did not remember meeting her, but she remembered me quiet vividly. We had met briefly for ten minutes one morning in Leon. I had shared with her why I was hiking. I had said I was trying to discern God's will for my life, and immediately she had said she was a recovering Catholic in response to my story. Now, as we sat in the albergue talking, I knew that the wall she had put up when we had met in Leon was not what her heart really desired. I knew that if I wanted to avoid someone, I would not engage that person in conversation or remind him or her that we had already met. I went to the grocery store and pharmacy and then headed down to church for Mass. As I entered the church, I saw the woman sitting on the back pew. I sat next to her, and she invited me to join her for dinner, which I agreed to. She left prior to Mass starting. I was nourished through the Mass, and then I joined the woman for dinner.

I shared my story about my hike that morning, walking on the mountain, praying the rosary, and seeing the sun so brilliant as it rose and about how it reminded me of the Miracle of Fatima. The woman then shared that, when she was a child, the message of Fatima had a profound impact on her, but she did not know why, and that she had always had a love for Mary. By that point, it would seem I would understand that God works in mysterious ways. And when we allow Him to use us, He does just that. But once again, God completely surprised me. In the past when I have spoken to people who were Catholic once upon a time, usually one of their issues with the Catholic Church is the way the church shows honor to Mary. Yet, here my story that God had me share with this woman allowed us to begin our dinner conversation on common ground.

The conversation was yet another gift from God. We both shared our life stories and listened to one another in true love. After a while, I felt called to ask her why she had called herself a recovering Catholic. She opened up and shared her story about what had hurt her and why she had left the faith. After a while, another woman whom I had felt called to talk to on this trip left her own table and joined our table. The three of us stayed at that restaurant talking about faith and life for hours, and we almost missed the lockout time of our albergue. This was one of the many great conversations God allowed me to be part of along the Camino. I knew that God had chosen to use me to place a little water on the seeds in those two women's hearts (that He had someone else plant long ago). I could see that both of the women were thirsting for God, though they were not aware that they were longing for Him. I never saw either of the women after that night, but I am confident that God will continue to place people in their lives and they will both return to Him, His love, and His church.

Scripture Meditation: 1 Corinthians 3:5-9

What is Apollos, after all, and what is Paul? Ministers through whom you became believers, just as the Lord assigned each one. I planted, Apollos watered, but God caused the growth. Therefore, neither the one who plants nor the one who waters is anything, but only God, who causes the growth. The one who plants and the one who waters are equal, and each will receive wages in proportion to his labor. For we are God's co-workers; you are God's field, God's building.

Reflection:

God has used many people to plant seeds of faith in my life. What have some of the seeds been?

In what way has God used Mary to water the seeds of faith in my life?

How can I help water the seeds of faith in people around me?

As someone who has spent a good number of years teaching children and teens religious education, I can tell you that I try really hard to make sure I am planting seeds of faith. In the same way, through my conversations with friends, as well as my social media posts, I try to give water to the different seeds planted long ago by someone else. But no matter how many seeds I plant or how much water I try to give, only God can cause a seed to react to the water and allow a person to grow. In the same sense, any good seed I plant or any good water I give a person comes from God.

Lesson 35:

As I walked down a steep decline, I could feel pain specifically in my knees, and I realized how important my knees were to my entire body. On this trip, I had noticed the various parts of my body more than normal. I never realized how much of my body I took for granted. To simply walk I have not only taken my feet and legs for granted but also my knees, my hips, my toes, and my ankles, to name a few. I think the same is true in our church; we never realize which members we have taken for granted until they are missing.

In our church, we often recognize the pastor, but we fail to recognize the person in charge of the sound system that allows us to hear the words of our pastor. We recognize the guest speaker that comes to present at a spiritual retreat, but we fail to recognize the committee that hosted the retreat. It is only when the microphone has a high-pitch squeak that we notice the sound person is absent. We each have a role to play within our church community, and if one of us is missing, the community is missing something: the gifts of time, talent, and treasure.

My bachelor's degree is in emergency management, and during Hurricane Katrina, I served as a shelter manager for a thirty-day period until we closed the shelter. Every single morning the local newspapers greeted me before 6:00 a.m. for a shelter update and the story of the day. In addition, we had regional camera crews coming to obtain stories, as well as an international news crew from Germany. The media always wanted to interview me for the larger story, as well as interview a few of the hurricane survivors for their personal stories. Although I was a volunteer at the shelter that was constantly in the spotlight, the reality is we had over twelve hundred volunteers in that thirty-day period, supporting that shelter with time and talent. We also had a number of people supporting the shelter with their treasure.

No organization or business that is to have a global impact can function on a single person unless that person is God. It takes many people using their skills and abilities together to serve a common goal. God does not need us, but He has chosen to use us, and throughout time, we have seen Him working with groups of people and not just one person, though God clearly picks one to be the leader. When Jesus came to set up God's Kingdom on earth, He chose twelve apostles, but He also brought in seventy-two disciples. Just like biblical times, Christians today have a chance to serve side by side with their brothers and sisters in Christ to work in the Lord's vineyard.

When we give our time, talent, and treasure to serve God and the Church, we need to do it for that reason alone: to serve God and the Church. We should never serve expecting recognition or praise from our Pastor but solely as a gift to God. While children, some of us learned to write thank-you notes when we received gifts, but thank-you notes should never be expected. If the note is expected, then the gift is not really a gift. Please understand that I am not against thank you notes or parents teaching their children to be polite. A true gift is given with no strings attached, which means we give gifts without expecting anything in return from the recipients. Many people get upset when they do not receive thank-you cards after giving gifts. When we give gifts of time, talent, or treasure, we need to do so with pure hearts, with no hidden motives or desires attached to the gifts other than love. I think we all can recognize those who serve to be recognized and those who serve to love. Hopefully, we each serve to love and use the gifts we have been given to serve.

Scripture Meditation: 1 Corinthian 12:4-27

There are different kinds of spiritual gifts but the same Spirit; there are different forms of service but the same Lord; there are different workings but the same God who produces all of them in everyone. To each individual the manifestation of the Spirit is given for some benefit. To one is given through the Spirit the expression of wisdom; to another the expression of knowledge according to the same Spirit; to another faith by the same Spirit; to another gifts of healing by the one Spirit; to another mighty deeds; to another prophecy; to another discernment of spirits; to another varieties of tongues; to another interpretation of tongues. But one and the same Spirit produces all of these, distributing them individually to each person as he wishes. As a body is one though it has many parts, and all the parts of the body, though many, are one body, so also Christ. For in one Spirit we were all baptized into one body, whether Jews or Greeks, slaves or free persons, and we were all given to drink of one Spirit. Now the body is not a single part, but many. If a foot should say, "Because I am not a hand I do not belong to the body," it does not for this reason belong any less to the body. Or if an ear should say, "Because I am not an eye I do not belong to the body," it does not for this reason belong any less to the body. If the whole body were an eye, where would the hearing be? If the whole body were hearing, where would the sense of smell be? But as it is, God placed the parts, each one of them, in the body as he intended. If they were all one part, where would the body be? But as it is, there are many parts, yet one body. The eye cannot say to the hand, "I do not need you," nor again the head to the feet, "I do not need you." Indeed, the parts of the body that seem to be weaker are all the more necessary, and those parts of the body that we consider less honorable we surround with greater honor, and our less presentable parts are treated with greater propriety, whereas our more presentable parts do not need this. But God has so constructed the body as to give greater honor to a part that is without it, so that there may be no division in the body, but that the parts may have the same concern for one another. If [one] part suffers, all the parts suffer with it; if one part is honored, all the parts share its joy. Now you are Christ's body, and individually parts of it.

Reflection:

What gifts of my time, talent, and treasure do I contribute to God and in what ways?

What role do I play in my church community?

Do I ever get jealous of the roles that others play?

On the Camino, I came to realize and appreciate each of the various parts that make up my body. Whenever a part of the body was underperforming, another member of the body stepped up. As I came down the mountain and the impact from the decline hurt my knees, I noticed how my arms were able to alleviate some of the pain on my knees by taking some of the weight with the use of the walking poles. When I look around my church, I see many people who work together to serve God and His mission here on earth. In the same way, when one member of our community stumbles, the entire body does not fall down, but instead, other members quickly work to help that member until the member is able to return to his or her former service. We are one body in Christ, and we will never be alone.

Lesson 36:

Many of the businesses in the towns along the Camino exist solely for the pilgrims. Many of the business owners I met along the Camino had servants' hearts, and they charged modest prices for their services, as if they were part of a ministry instead of a business. Of course, many other people operated businesses that intended to make money. For them, if they could sell something to a pilgrim and make a profit, they offered it. In addition to various supplies that would make my experience easier, I also saw flyers advertising to have backpacks transported for hikers.

On the first day, as I walked through the French Pyrenees in the rain, sleet, and wind, I felt pain throughout my entire body. Then I prayed, and I accepted that small cross. An excerpt from my journal on the second night of walking says, "As I lay in bed, I feel the pain. After walking the trail, it is like my body shut down, and I became a ninety-five-year-old woman on a walker. Some other pilgrims have their bags shipped by bus from one town to the next, and one of the fellow pilgrims, upon seeing how slowly I walked up the stairs, told me that I should do it. One of the brothers I was hiking with told me not to do it, and I told him I would have to see what God has to say." The reason the brother told me not to (and I agreed) was because I saw this as a true pilgrimage, and I wanted to offer up any hardship to the Lord. At the same time, as I walked up the stairs as if I was using a walker, I was unsure if I would be able to walk the entire Camino. My journal continues, "The first Mass reading began, '*With their patience worn out by the journey, the people complained against God and Moses,*' and immediately upon hearing these words, I knew

I would carry my bag and offer it up to the Lord." Oh the irony; this occurred on the Feast of the Exaltation of the Cross!

That was the early part of the Camino, and if other pilgrims chose to send their bags ahead to the next town by transport, that did not bother me, because we each walked the Camino our own way. As I got closer to the end, during the last one hundred kilometers, I began noticing all the signage, not just at the albergues but also along the trail for backpack transport, as well as taxi service. The majority of pilgrims on the Camino will only hike the last one hundred kilometers, because many people do not have the time available or the health to walk the entire Camino. Many Camino hospitaleros referred to the pilgrims that hike only the last portion as tourist pilgrims and would joke saying, "The pilgrims with little bags and big shells." Many of those tourist pilgrims, like me, had not trained physically. The pain of walking with a backpack all day surprised them. The companies that offered taxi services or bag transport intentionally played on the fact that humans often take the easy way out. We are not conditioned to like pain, and in reality, we learn to run away from pain.

Although we have a natural instinct to take the easy way out, it is the hard times and the challenges we face that often create character. If we choose to take the easy way out when faced with challenges then our characters usually flee from difficult stuff. However, if we face challenges head on, then our characters are usually of determination and ability to confront difficult situations. I could have justified sending my bag based on my injuries, but the fact that I kept walking with my bag strengthened my faith in God, as well as my will power. If we always take the easy ways out, we will miss golden opportunities.

Scripture Meditation: Matthew 16:24

Then Jesus said to his disciples, "Whoever wishes to come after me must deny himself, take up his cross, and follow me.

Reflection:

What crosses do I currently struggle to accept?

How do I respond normally when faced with a cross?

The next time you face a challenge, I encourage you to embrace that challenge and not take the easy way out. See that challenge as an opportunity from God to grow and learn. Taking the easy way might seem good at that moment, but it will not do you any good later in life.

Lesson 37:

It was not a coincidence that, during my forty days on the Camino, I attended three different funeral Masses or that the Camino de Santiago is known as the longest cemetery in the world. After I attended my third funeral Mass, I thought about my pilgrimage and the graces that God was granting me.

The first part of my trip was the most physically demanding, and I was constantly praying and asking God for strength. It was during that part that I offered the pain as a very small atonement to God for my sins, as well as a gift of my love. As Jesus had embraced the cross for me, I now embraced this very small cross for Jesus. Every day as I walked and prayed, I thought of how small this sacrifice compared to my lifetime of sins. Then during the middle section, the physically demanding mountains were gone and, with that, all the thoughts of my sins. As I walked I was not thinking of my past or my future, but instead I was just silent. I had retreated to my inner-self, spent the time withdrawn from others, and focused my thoughts on hearing from God. Then as my pilgrimage came close to the end, I began noticing my thoughts drift to my future. What will I do when I reach Santiago? After Santiago, where will I go? When I return to the states, what will I do for my career? Where will I live? What about my vocation? Am I any closer toward which way to go? Those thoughts and so many more came into my head, and I would spend the time talking with God about each of those questions to see what He thought I should do.

Then I attended the third funeral Mass on the last part of my trip, and I understood clearly that I am not promised tomorrow. The Bible verse I had read in adoration in Santo Domingo, which had humbled me, now returned to me but in a different context. I thought of the man who had built barns to store up his wealth and then died on that very night. We should look to our futures and think about how we can use the gifts God has given us to be good stewards of the resources we have. We must also realize that we will not live forever. Part of this experience for me is being mindful that the future I really need to be planning for is getting into heaven. The future should not be about what house I will live in, how much money I will have, and all those other details that so often trap us. The funeral that night was a good reminder to plan for the eternal and not the temporary. We have no clue of the length of our earthly lives, but we do know our eternal lives are forever, and hopefully, we know where we want to spend that eternity. After all, there are only two options!

Scripture Meditation: Luke 12:20-21

But God said to him, 'You fool, this night your life will be demanded of you; and the things you have prepared, to whom will they belong?' Thus will it be for the one who stores up treasure for himself but is not rich in what matters to God."

Reflection:

What do I think about when planning for the future?

What do I worry about and how can I give it over to God?

What future am I planning for: retirement or heaven?

I love the Mass, but I have a special place in my heart for both Baptismal and funeral Masses. In the Baptismal Mass, as a community, we stand and retake our Baptismal oath, but we also agree, as a community, to help raise the child. Then, as a community, we once again come together at a funeral Mass to celebrate the life of the person, as well as to say farewell to his or her body, the tabernacle that carried around the Lord. It is at these two Masses that I remember we are all linked together and the reason we are here on this earth. At the Baptismal Mass, I remember my promise to God, and at the funeral Mass, I remember that, at any point, I might die. Thus, there is an urgency to constantly fulfill my Baptismal promise.

Lesson 38:

My time on the Camino was coming to an end; I was approaching the town where I would spend my final night on the Camino prior to arriving in Santiago on the following day. The closer I got to Santiago, the more I realized the amazing experience that God had enriched my life with was coming to an end. I had mixed emotions about the excitement of being able to talk to and see my family and friends again, as well as the sadness that comes with the ending of a beautiful chapter in my life.

As I approached the town on a trail in the woods, on my right hand side, I watched a butterfly simply move along the path at the pace I was walking. The butterfly, the trees, and the natural beauty symbolized the amazing experience I had spent with God. And to my left, I heard the noise of the interstate that was passing about ten feet away from me. That interstate, constructed by man, symbolized the noise that I had walked away from during my pilgrimage and the very real distractions that I would face upon ending my pilgrimage.

At the last monastery I stayed at, I remember thinking about all the Saints who had come from religious communities. The Saints that I look up to all belonged to religious communities. Some Saints had chosen the committed single life or married life, but for me, the Saints who have helped me grow spiritually from their writings had all chosen the vocation as a consecrated religious. I do not think the majority of people who enter religious life are any holier than people who choose to marry or live a committed single life. But I think people who choose the religious life, over time, will find it easier to grow in holy virtues than people who have chosen a committed single or married life. As religious people, they attend daily Mass, participate multiple times in community prayer, and make time for silent reflection, prayer, and meditation, allowing them to grow in faith. It is easier in the world of religious life to constantly pursue God, because the preset schedule encourages them to do just that. On the other hand, a committed single or married person can do everything a religious person can do, but must choose to do it every day. Unfortunately, they often lack the support that a religious community can give.

On my journey, I had been able to attend daily Mass more frequently than when I had a career. I read the scripture more often and participated in vespers and morning prayers for the first time in my life. I had more silence than at any other time in my life. Soon I would be entering back into the world and would have to work very hard to avoid the noise of life, like the interstate that was trying to distract me. I had enjoyed the silence and my time to commune with God that I had received on my pilgrimage. For me, part of my experience had been the forty-day aspect, which modern research tells me should have created a habit. I hoped that silence and prayer time would be something I would continue upon returning to the world of noise that bombards us all. A lot of times, we attend a retreat or workshop and leave on a spiritual high, just like my high from the Camino, and we are ready to recommit our lives. Over time, that high goes down, and soon we find we are no better off than we were prior to the retreat. We want to make retreats part of our daily lives as well as do mini-retreats throughout the day to constantly help us stay on that spiritual high.

Creating our own daily retreat is not difficult, but if we are going to do it, we need to commit. Maybe before we take showers in the morning, we could spend time in prayer and read a chapter of the Bible. Then during lunch breaks, we could go away from other people to pray and meditate on a spiritual work. At the end of workdays, we could sit in our cars and meditate on the way we saw God working in our lives during the day. Then as we get ready for bed, we could give God thanks, examine our conscious to see where we fell short, and pray for God's grace to help us overcome our faults. Each of these mini-retreats takes fewer than fifteen minutes but could have a powerful impact. Of course, we could also find time to attend daily Mass, pray in Adoration, or even begin praying the Liturgy of the Hours in front of the tabernacle. To make these mini-retreats a reality, all we need to do is cut down on the noise, turn off our phones, and turn our minds over to God.

I have been truly blessed to have heard the Holy Spirit talking to me on my pilgrimage more than ever in my life, and it was not because all of sudden the Holy Spirit began talking to me. It was because I gave the Holy Spirit the opportunity to talk through the silence, and I was listening. That is something I want to keep. It has been amazing watching the Holy Spirit work for me and through me, and I will do whatever it takes to keep this pilgrimage alive in me.

Scripture Meditation: Luke 10:38-42

As they continued their journey he entered a village where a woman whose name was Martha welcomed him. She had a sister named Mary [who] sat beside the Lord at his feet listening to him speak. Martha, burdened with much serving, came to him and said, "Lord, do you not care that my sister has left me by myself to do the serving? Tell her to help me." The Lord said to her in reply, "Martha, Martha, you are anxious and worried about many things. There is need of only one thing. Mary has chosen the better part and it will not be taken from her."

Reflection:

What distractions keep me from God?

What am I willing to do to create mini-retreats throughout my day to stay on my spiritual high?

If I could create a daily schedule filled with little opportunities to stay connected to God, what would that look like?

I love the story of Mary and Martha, because I think we all have a good amount of Martha in us. We are servers, yet we need to learn to slow down and focus on what is most important. We have to let the distractions of decisions we need to make wait while we simply sit with our Lord. If we never spend the time to sit with the Lord, how will we ever know what His will is for us?

Lesson 39:

It was about day thirty that my groin pulled, which caused nonstop pain. Every incline and decline hurt. I could only take small steps, and they got smaller. I went from walking four to six kilometers an hour, depending on the terrain, to only two and a half kilometers on flat terrain. Bending my leg to get dressed, undressed, and in and out of the sleeping bag was excruciating. As I said earlier, God gave me the grace and strength to keep walking, and each day I walked with that twenty-seven-pound pack. So on day thirty-nine, I arrived at the albergue after the physically hardest day, because the pain kept getting worse each day I continued walking. I arrived in the town about twenty kilometers away from Santiago, and a German girl I had met a few nights back greeted me and showed me to the albergue where she was staying. I showered, hung my clothes up to dry on the line, and got into my bed to elevate my foot. I was under the covers because I was very cold. I was a bit sick, and the rain over the past few days kept me cold.

From a flyer I saw, I knew the town offered a Mass at 6:30 p.m., but I never saw the church on my way into town, and our hospitalero did not speak English. In my head, I gave the excuse that I attended Mass the day before and that on the following day I would be in Santiago to attend Mass, so I could just skip dinner and Mass and stay in bed. Then I thought, "No," the entire reason I was there was to grow closer to God, and nothing brought me closer to God than the Mass. So, I got up, put on my coat, and began the pilgrim shuffle out of the albergue. As I went outside, it was raining, and I gave the excuse that I was already cold and sick and would get wet and possibly sicker. I told myself that I should just get back in bed. So, I turned around and headed inside, where I told myself that was just another excuse. I grabbed my poncho, put it over my coat, and again began the pilgrim shuffle back out the door. I stopped at a restaurant and asked for the church. The fellow pointed down the hill and spoke in Spanish. So, I began walking down the hill in the direction he pointed. The pain was great, and I did not see a church anywhere in sight. As I got further away from my albergue, I thought of having to walk back up the hill. So, I told myself my third excuse: that I did not see the church and I was tired and injured—just go back. Then I cast aside that thought, flagged down a tractor, and asked, "De donde Iglesia?" The driver pointed in the opposite direction, and I walked a good way to the church.

As soon as I got inside the church, I kneeled to pray. I realized those excuses were really from the devil; he was trying to keep me from attending the Mass. About ten nights prior, as I had talked with Texas and his dad, the dad had shared that the closer we got to Santiago the more we would be under spiritual warfare, because the devil does not want us making pilgrimages to grow in our faith or to help others grow. I smiled, knowing I had overcome these three very small but very real temptations to skip Mass. The Mass was in Italian, but what I heard during the homily was that many people walk fast on the Camino and take photos or grab stamps, but they miss the reason for the Camino: Mass—the most important thing. As I left the church that evening, I noticed I was taking longer strides than I had in days, and I did not feel the groin pain as badly as I had only an hour before. I smiled, knowing how good God is and that I was able to overcome all the temptations placed in my way. I literally gave God a high five in the air and just felt on fire with God; it was a beautiful moment for me.

Scripture Meditation: Matthew 4: 1-11

Then Jesus was led by the Spirit into the desert to be tempted by the devil. He fasted for forty days and forty nights, and afterwards he was hungry. The tempter approached and said to him, "If you are the Son of God, command that these stones become loaves of bread." He said in reply, "It is written: 'One does not live by bread alone, but by every word that comes forth from the mouth of God.'" Then the devil took him to the holy city, and made him stand on the parapet of the temple, and said to him, "If you are the Son of God, throw yourself down. For it is written: 'He will command his angels concerning you' and 'with their hands they will support you, lest you dash your foot against a stone.'" Jesus answered him, "Again it is written, 'You shall not put the Lord, your God, to the test.'" Then the devil took him up to a very high mountain, and showed him all the kingdoms of the world in their magnificence, and he said to him, "All these I shall give to you, if you will prostrate yourself and worship me." At this, Jesus said to him, "Get away, Satan! It is written: 'The Lord, your God, shall you worship and him alone shall you serve.'" Then the devil left him and, behold, angels came and ministered to him.

Reflection:

Looking at my life, when was a time that I was under spiritual warfare?

What temptations has the devil put before me today?

Do I think that God will ever allow the devil to attack me beyond my limits?

I have come to believe that when I was choosing to live a life apart from God, the devil never needed to worry about my soul. I was doing enough damage without the devil having to lift a finger. But when I consciously chose to live my life for God and strove to do His will, I found that the devil suddenly became interested and began coming at me. Sometimes the devil came in a form I was able to recognize; other times I did not recognize the form he used. This is why we must always be on guard and cling to Jesus to avoid being tricked by the devil. The three excuses seemed very small and insignificant, yet it was a major spiritual victory for me. What spiritual victories in your own life do you need to celebrate with God?

Lesson 40:

The anticipation grew each step on my final day walking into Santiago. Upon arrival at the Cathedral, I entered and walked around the historic cathedral and then sought out a Priest for reconciliation. I had made a confession forty-two days prior in Lourdes, but on my Camino, I had spent time thinking of my failures in life and the sins I had committed. And although I had previously confessed my sins, I found that I had failed to allow God's grace to truly forgive me, as I was unable to accept the forgiveness. None of the Priests could speak English, and my heart sank. I walked into the side chapel, where Adoration of our Lord was taking place, and I kneeled to pray. I had come to peace on my Camino but desired confession so I could fully allow God's love and absolution to blanket me through the Sacrament of Reconciliation. It was then that I decided I would write down all my sins as I prayed in Adoration. I would then leave the church to find Internet service and translate my confession into Spanish so that I could come back and confess my sins in Spanish.

After writing down all my sins, I kneeled there like the tax collector in Luke 18:10-13. "*Two people went up to the temple area to pray; one was a Pharisee and the other was a tax collector. The Pharisee took up his position and spoke this prayer to himself, 'O God, I thank you that I am not like the rest of humanity— greedy, dishonest, adulterous—or even like this tax collector. I fast twice a week, and I pay tithes on my whole income.' But the tax collector stood off at a distance and would not even raise his eyes to heaven but beat his breast and prayed, 'O God, be merciful to me a sinner.'*"

After that, I was feeling better, so I left the church, walked around to find Internet, and stumbled upon a church behind the Cathedral. Unlike the Cathedral filled with pilgrims and tourists, this church was empty, and I went in to pray all alone. After an hour, a nun entered and began setting up the altar. She motioned for me to get a book at the front, so I went up and got two books to participate in night vespers. The bell rang, and at least forty nuns began filling in their seats on both sides of the altar. That evening, night vespers were truly beautiful. It was my first time operating out of a Liturgy of the Hours, and even though it was in Spanish, I was able to follow along using the two books. After night vespers, the nuns left the church, I knelt down to pray, and I began crying. I had originally done the pilgrimage to figure out what vocation God was calling me to, and although I was hearing God talk to me about many topics, He had not told me His will for my vocation. The pilgrimage had given me many mixed messages about which vocation to do, and I had learned that God's will and timeline are far better than any plans I could make. So, I had accepted I would wait until He was ready for me. I was not crying because I did not know my vocation but because I was not worthy. God has given me so many gifts and so many chances, yet I have failed. I have deliberately chosen things that were against God, yet He kept lifting me up and bringing me to new heights. I knew the feeling of being not worthy was not coming from God, and I knew what I had to do.

I returned to the Cathedral, went to the door of the Sacristy, and began asking every Priest that was exiting, "Habla English?" I must have looked desperate with tears in my eyes, because finally, one of the staff members recognized me from earlier that day and motioned for me to enter the Sacristy. A Priest from America came and said he would be happy to hear my confession. We went around to the corner to the confessional, I knelt facing him, and began my confession, and the tears would not hold back. The lights in the Cathedral were turning off, but Father stayed there, and it was a beautiful confession. I was finally ready to receive God's forgiveness for my past failures, and then something unexpected happened. After I shared with the Priest everything that weighed on my heart, he offered me God's forgiveness, and once again, God spoke to me. Through the Priest in that confessional, God gave me what to do next.

What the Priest shared with me matched so many of the other signs that God had given me. I knew leaving my pilgrimage that my focus would be on the evangelization of God's people. God has called each one of us to help rebuild His Church. Saint Francis of Assisi answered that call eight hundred years ago, and we, too, must decide if we will answer that call and what that will look like. For there are many ways to rebuild His Church, and we each must use the gifts we have been given to rebuild His Church. I invite you, my friends, for your final reflection to spend some time in prayer asking God where He wants you and how you can help rebuild His Church. May God bless you and guide you all the days of your life.

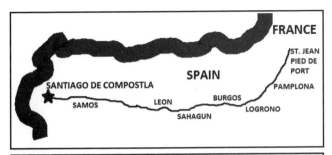

FRANCE

SPAIN

ST. JEAN
PIED DE
PORT

PAMPLONA

SANTIAGO DE COMPOSTLA

SAMOS   LEON   BURGOS   LOGRONO

SAHAGUN

Spiritual Lessons along the Camino

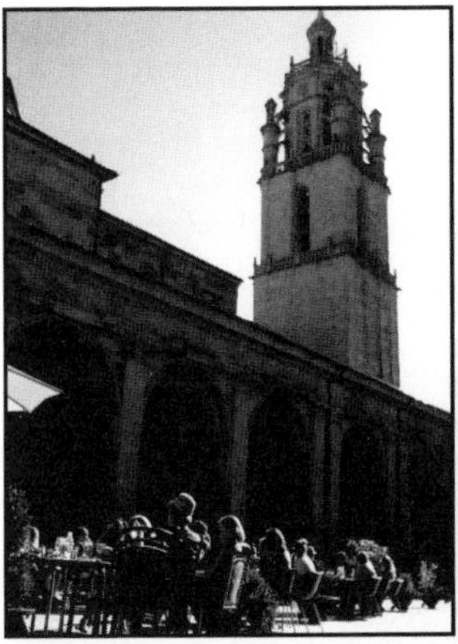
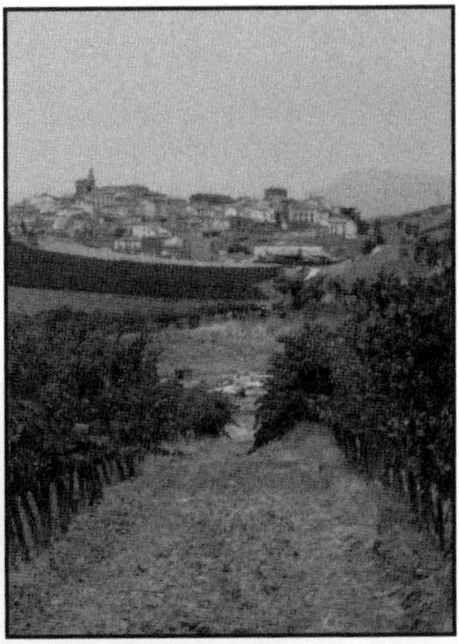
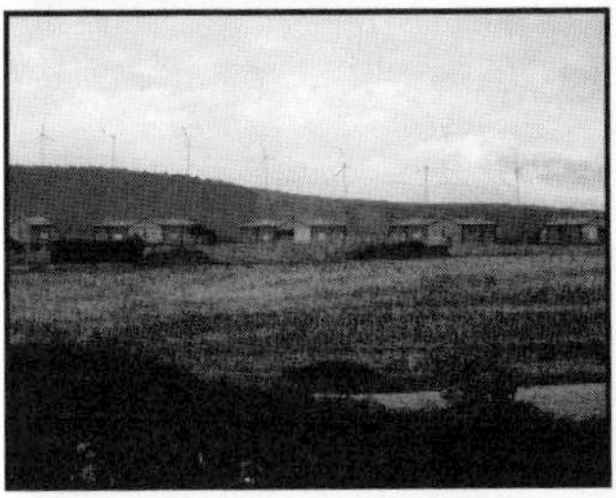
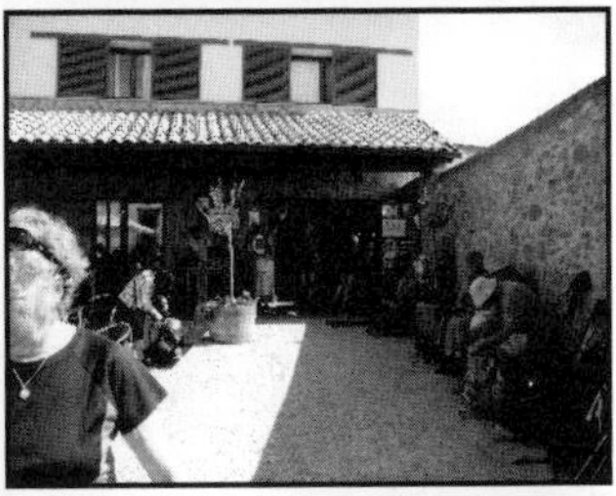
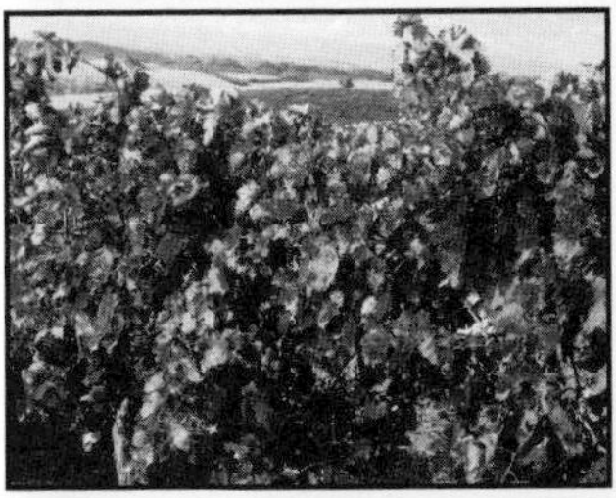
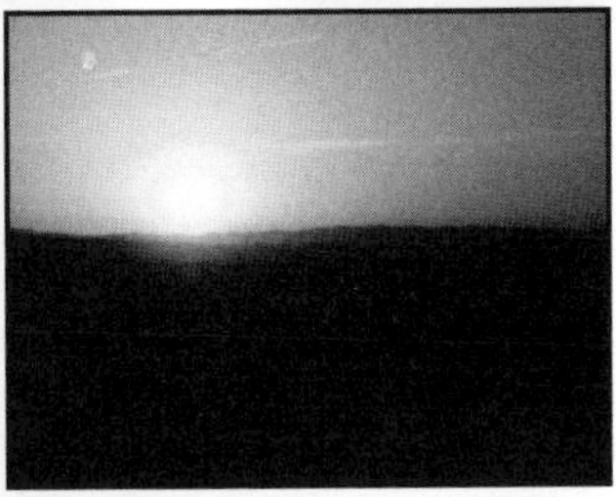
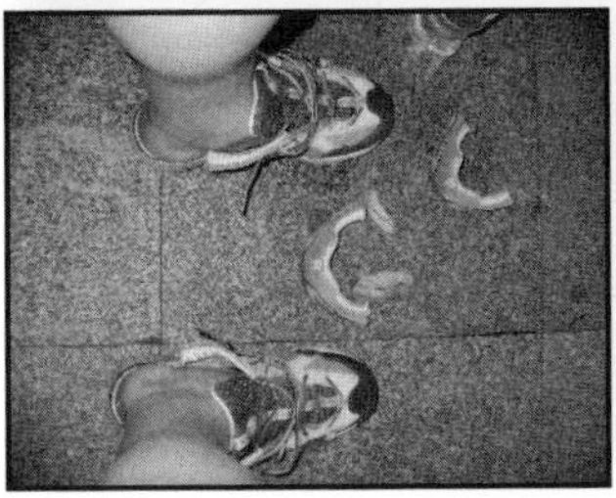
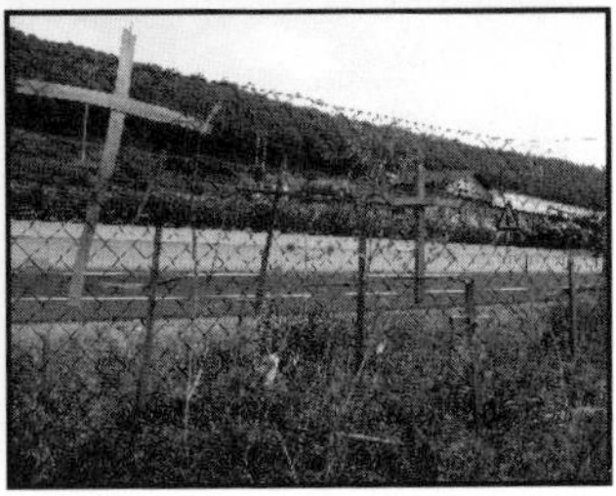

Spiritual Lessons along the Camino

Spiritual Lessons along the Camino

Spiritual Lessons along the Camino

Scripture Meditation: Psalm 23

The Lord is my shepherd; there is nothing I lack. In green pastures you let me graze; to safe waters you lead me; you restore my strength. You guide me along the right path for the sake of your name. Even when I walk through a dark valley, I fear no harm for you are at my side; your rod and staff give me courage You set a table before me as my enemies watch; You anoint my head with oil; my cup overflows. Only goodness and love will pursue me all the days of my life; I will dwell in the house of the Lord for years to come.

BUEN CAMINO